Praise for the first edition of AN INSIDER'S GUIDE TO THE UN

"A short-order account of how the organization works in the glare of its public profile and in the shadow of its secret negotiations."—*Times* (London)

"This unique book combines a solid guide to the workings of the United Nations with illuminating insights from credible and serious experts."—Barbara Crossette, former *New York Times* UN bureau chief

"[A] wonderful insider's guide . . . packed with great information." —John McLaughlin, host, *McLaughlin Group*

"One of the best reference guides for those inside and outside the UN system."—IPS UN Journal (Inter Press Service)

"Practical observations, . . . combined with Fasulo's map of the UN's domains, will help Model UN participants."—*Booklist*

"Great education for newcomers as well as long-timers at the UN." —Mark Malloch Brown, former UN deputy-secretary-general

AN INSIDER'S GUIDE TO THE UN

AN INSIDER'S GUIDE

TO

THE

Second edition

LINDA FASULO

Yale University Press / New Haven and London

Set in Scala type by Keystone Typesetting, Inc.
Printed in the United States of America.

Library of Congress Cataloging-in-Publication Data
Fasulo, Linda M.
An insider's guide to the UN / Linda Fasulo. — 2nd ed.
    p.   cm.
Includes bibliographical references and index.
ISBN 978-0-300-14197-9 (paperbound : alk. paper)
1. United Nations—Popular works. I. Title.
JZ4984.6.F37 2009
341.23—dc22
2008052231

A catalogue record for this book is available from the British
Library.

This paper meets the requirements of ANSI/NISO
Z39.48-1992 (Permanence of Paper).
It contains 30 percent postconsumer waste (PCW) and is
certified by the Forest Stewardship Council (FSC).

10 9 8 7 6 5 4 3 2

For my son, Alex, my husband, Rob, and my mother, Mary

CONTENTS

ACKNOWLEDGMENTS

This book and its second edition would not have been possible without the encouragement, advice, and support of many people. To all of the diplomats, UN officials, analysts, and experts whom I have interviewed, I express my sincere thanks for their interest and participation as "Insiders" in this book. They include UN Secretary-General Ban Ki-moon, former UN Deputy Secretary-General Lord Mark Malloch Brown, Secretary of State Madeleine Albright; Ambassadors Munir Akram, John Bolton, John Danforth, Richard Holbrooke, Colin Keating, Zalmay Khalilzad, David Malone, John Negroponte, Nancy Soderberg, and Danilo Türk; and UN officials and experts Shepard Forman, Jeffrey Laurenti, William Luers, Edward Luck, Arieh Neuer, Shashi Tharoor, Brian Urquhart, and Ruth Wedgwood, who all graciously shared their unique and invaluable personal insights and experiences.

Over the past seven years, from preparation of the first edition, to the paperback edition, and then this second edition, it has been a consistent pleasure to work with the wonderful professionals at Yale University Press. This includes the editorial and executive divisions as well as the marketing, sales, and publicity departments. One could not have asked for a better publishing experience. Thanks especially to

Bill Frucht, John Kulka, Keith Condon, Jonathan Brent, Tina Weiner, Jane Comins, Laura Jones Dooley, Nancy Moore, Liz Pelton, Joseph Calamia, Debra Bozzi, and Peter Sims. And thanks to Yale University Press for its generous financial backing for this project, without which this book would not have been possible.

For supplemental grants provided during preparation of the first edition, I am grateful to the UN Foundation, in particular Tim Wirth, Melinda Kimble, and Phyllis Cuttino, and the Rockefeller Brothers Fund, specifically President Stephen Heintz. In addition, I thank the World Affairs Council of Philadelphia, especially Buntzie Ellis Churchill, Claudia McBride, and Margaret Lonzetta, for their enthusiastic sponsorship and continued interest in this project. Warm thanks go to Kirsten Plonner, my researcher, for her devoted day-to-day work in seeing the first edition to completion. To my longtime friend and colleague Bill Zeisel, PhD, of QED Associates, I thank him for his continued role in this project and his exceptionally discerning eye in the preparation of the manuscript for both editions. I thank my son, Alex, for his technical savvy and research assistance and my mother, Mary, for her help in transcribing recorded interviews in this edition. In addition, I thank Esther Margolis for introducing me to Yale University Press.

I also express my appreciation to my friends and colleagues at the UN, NBC News, and National Public Radio who gave encouragement along the way. And throughout this long experience, my family has been remarkably patient, enthusiastic, and supportive. For this I am incredibly appreciative.

A WORD TO THE READER

Working as a news correspondent at the United Nations has given me a firsthand perspective on one of the world's most high profile and important organizations. Nowhere else in the world can you watch an international group of diplomats, officials, and experts discuss the great challenges of our day and make decisions that can affect our lives for years to come. Curbing international terrorism, deploying peacekeepers, combating diseases like malaria and AIDS, promoting human rights and development, and trying to bring rogue nations like North Korea to account are only a few of the big issues the UN can address in a year.

At the UN, before the day's decisions have been voted on, the agenda has been set, the members have prepared themselves, disagreements have played out in relative privacy, and the public sees a polished performance. Many onlookers will accept this performance at face value and never give it another thought. For those who want to know more, who ask how the decisions were negotiated and reached and what their chances are for making a lasting impact, I have written this book, relying on my personal observations as well as the experiences and insights of other insiders.

Flags at UN headquarters in New York City. UN Photo/Andrea Brizzi

A World of Change

When I began writing the first edition of the book, the world was still reeling from the terrorist attacks of September 11, 2001. Since then, the world has changed, and so has the United Nations. Threats like international terrorism and the proliferation of nuclear weapons weigh ever more heavily on minds around the world. The UN has taken a more active role against terrorists and in the process has itself become a victim of terrorist attacks.

Other global issues such as climate change are also pressing forward in global public awareness and in the UN. The pace of globalization has quickened and with it a growing sense that nations are interdependent and interrelated. Growing globalization makes an organization like the UN even more visible and useful. As a result, the UN is experiencing a surge in activity. It is being asked to provide humanitarian aid much more frequently than before, in response to natural and human-caused disasters like cyclones, tsunamis, famines, and civil wars. Peacekeeping has become a growth industry at the UN. Recent years have seen a big increase in the number of peacekeeping missions, and the concept of peacebuilding has been institutionalized through new offices and funds in the Secretariat. Understandably, the UN's general operations are experiencing a rapid budget escalation.

The key personalities have changed dramatically since 2001, with the departure, after two terms, of Secretary-General Kofi Annan, who had worked at the UN for many years before becoming secretary-general and thus was the consummate "insider," and the arrival of a lesser-known but well-accomplished South Korean diplomat, Ban Ki-moon, as successor in the post. Meanwhile, since 2001 the United States has appointed, in succession, four different men to the post of US ambassador.

Not all changes have been favorable for the UN. The organization is experiencing a growing rift between the affluent and less affluent countries, often called the North–South divide. The rift is glaring in the General Assembly, which is the UN's main deliberative body and provides a forum for all of the organization's 192 member states. The UN has also been rocked by scandal. The Oil-for-Food Programme (intended to help feed the Iraqi people after the first Gulf War in 1991) was abused by the Saddam Hussein regime in ways that also tarred the UN. This led to renewed efforts at reforming the UN to make it more transparent and effective.

Finally, change has marked the relationship between the United States and the UN. The contentiousness that erupted in the Security Council in 2003, when the United States and its allies sought backing for the invasion of Iraq, has been replaced by a much more amicable atmosphere. The United States remains the UN's single biggest financial supporter, and it is still perceived by many as the ultimate enforcer of international security. Nevertheless, US efforts to exert its influence in the UN are changing in the face of the North–South divide and the growing assertiveness of such nations as China and Russia.

A New Edition

Given these many changes, I was pleased when Yale University Press gave me the opportunity to update the book with a new edition. Once I began revising and updating, however, I found that the degree of change both inside and outside the UN has been so large that I had to rethink many of the chapters and write a new one—on climate change. I rearranged material to focus on issues of growing global prominence, such as the rule of law. As part of my research, I interviewed a dozen more UN insiders, each with his or her own unique knowledge and experience with the world body. These new voices, I hope, give the book a more complex flavor and greater depth of information and insight.

Despite all the changes, the UN remains the world's main global forum and coordinator of international efforts to address common problems and issues. This book is organized to provide the reader with a topical overview of the UN's organization, governing principles, and key functions It begins with historical background and moves quickly to the UN's chief executive officer, the secretary-general, and his main international counterpart, the US ambassador. After that come chapters on the UN's most prominent "principal organs," the Security Council, including its peacekeeping operations, and the General Assembly, along with an informal trip through the UN Village, that little corner of New York City populated by diplomats from all over the world. In the succeeding chapters, the book explores such global issues as international terrorism, nuclear proliferation, the rule of law and human rights, and climate change, as well as the state of UN reform and finances. A look at the many agencies and programs that carry out the UN's broad efforts in social and economic development, disaster relief, eradication of diseases, and reducing the trade in addictive drugs follows. The book ends with a personal tale by Shashi

Founding Date

The UN was established on October 24, 1945, when the UN Charter was ratified. Thus October 24 is celebrated every year as UN Day. President Franklin D. Roosevelt and Prime Minister Winston Churchill coined the name "United Nations," first used in the "Declaration by United Nations" on January 1, 1942.

Tharoor, one of the most "inside" of insiders, who began his UN career with the challenge of helping Vietnamese boat people find refuge after their harrowing escapes from the Asian mainland.

Great Expectations?

More than half a century ago, the United States and its allies in World War II created an international body that they hoped would enable nations to prosper and live peacefully with one another. When the war ended in 1945, the new organization began with enormous goodwill, moral support from all sides, and strong US leadership. The world waited to see if the UN could rectify the shortcomings of the League of Nations, its predecessor organization, which dissolved in the late 1930s, victim of totalitarian regimes and US indifference. Could it be the uniting force among the victorious nations, whose ideologies and political interests often seemed at odds?

The cold war soon replaced idealistic collaboration with power politics between the West and the East. From the late 1940s until the breakup of the Soviet Union in 1991, confrontation among the blocs defined most UN relationships, discussions, debates, programs, and activities. A whole generation grew up with an East-West mindset, whose ghost still surfaces at the UN and elsewhere, even while a new world is emerging. During these many decades, expectations about the UN changed, becoming either more realistic or more cynical, depending on the viewpoint. Today, although Americans do not expect the UN to solve the world's problems, at the least they would like it to be a more effective partner in dealing with the forces that are trans-forming our world.

In the face of rapid and wrenching change, we have to wonder how an international organization created nearly sixty-five years ago, in a very different world, can maintain its relevance and effectiveness to-day, let alone in the future. That is the UN's greatest challenge—one that the insiders who run the UN and its associated agencies, and the diplomats who represent its member nations, have also been asking. Most believe it can step up to the new challenges while reforming its own shortcomings, but that is by no means the unanimous view. What we can say with certainty is that the pervasive and seemingly impersonal forces of change in our modern world will need to be addressed by living, breathing people, not computer software or me-chanical robots. The UN is, above all, a place for people and a hotbed of the human factor. As one of my "insiders" says, people really do matter at the UN, and they act in a context full of illusion, opinion, perception, and emotion.

CHAPTER 1

Introducing the UN

[The UN] is an indispensable—and imperfect—forum that should be made more effective as a venue for collective action against terror and proliferation, climate change and genocide, poverty and disease.
—Barack Obama, president of the United States

The United Nations came into existence as a result of the most terrible war in history. During World War II, American president Franklin D. Roosevelt, British prime minister Winston Churchill, and the leaders of several other major combatant nations agreed that it was necessary to create a world organization that would help ensure the peace in future years. Their ideas are enshrined in the Preamble to the UN's Charter, which is one of its fundamental documents:

We the peoples of the United Nations determined
to save succeeding generations from the scourge of war, which
twice in our lifetime has brought untold sorrow to mankind, and
to reaffirm faith in fundamental human rights, in the dignity and
worth of the human person, in the equal rights of men and
women and of nations large and small, and

"We the Peoples," from a poster about the UN Charter. UN Photo/Milton Grant

to establish conditions under which justice and respect for the obligations arising from treaties and other sources of international law can be maintained, and

to promote social progress and better standards of life in larger freedom,

and for these ends

to practice tolerance and live together in peace with one another as good neighbors, and

to unite our strength to maintain international peace and security, and

to ensure, by the acceptance of principles and the institution of methods, that armed force shall not be used, save in the common interest, and

to employ international machinery for the promotion of the economic and social advancement of all peoples,

have resolved to combine our efforts to accomplish these aims

Accordingly, our respective Governments, through representatives assembled in the city of San Francisco, who have exhibited their full powers found to be in good and due form, have agreed to the present Charter of the United Nations and do hereby establish an international organization to be known as the United Nations.

As the Preamble declares, the world's peoples, acting through their representatives, seek to create a just and prosperous world through common action. It could hardly be simpler, and yet, after more than six decades of trying, we still live amid global insecurity and, in many places, injustice and suffering. And the UN itself is far from simple. It straddles the globe, operating in almost every nation on earth, and it has a bewildering variety of offices, programs, and personnel. Let's begin, then, with some basic points and language that will appear throughout the book.

The UN and the United States: It Takes Two to Tango

Americans do not expect the UN to solve all the world's problems, but polls suggest that they would nevertheless like it to be a more effective partner in dealing with the forces and threats changing our world. The central role of the United States in creating and supporting the UN gives it a special place in UN affairs and has led many insiders to remark on the close and sometimes contentious relationship between the two entities. "The United Nations has no better friend than America," declares Secretary-General Ban Ki-moon. Arguing from national polls, he says that "most Americans want US foreign policy to be conducted in partnership with the UN. They understand that working together is in the best interest of the United States, the United Nations, and, most importantly, the peoples of the world."

An eminent diplomat who served under the Clinton administration as US ambassador to the UN from 1999 to 2001 offers a similar analysis. "I need to underscore repeatedly that the UN is only as good as the US commitment," says Richard Holbrooke, who negotiated the Dayton Accords, ending the war in Bosnia in 1995. "The UN cannot succeed if the US does not support it."

Another UN insider, speaking from a very different background, agrees with Holbrooke's assessment. Mark Malloch Brown spent many years running one of the UN's major agencies before becoming the deputy secretary-general during the last year of Kofi Annan's tenure as secretary-general. From this perch Malloch Brown gained a deep appreciation of the importance of the United States in almost all aspects of the UN's work. "You can't have an effective UN without very strong American engagement in the organization," he says. "The US has to be there in a strong leadership role."

The US domestic political establishment has often included highly placed experts and advisers to who favor a go-it-alone foreign policy, and for them the UN sometimes seems a greater hindrance than help. The dominant view during the past half-century, however, has been for the US government to cooperate with and enable the UN as much as possible, as long as it doesn't threaten fundamental American interests. President Barack Obama is on record as saying that "no country has a greater stake in a strong United Nations than the United States. The United States benefits from a global institution intended to advance the rule of law, the peaceful resolution of disputes, effective collective security, humanitarian relief, development, and respect for human rights." Madeleine Albright, US secretary of state under President Clinton during his second term, argues that the United States does not have the choice of acting "only through the UN or only alone." Rather, she says, "we want—and need—both options. So in diplomacy, an instrument like the UN will be useful in some situations, useless in others, and extremely valuable in getting the whole job done." The UN can help make the world a better place, she continues, and this is to our advantage because we know that "desperation is a parent to violence, that democratic principles are often among the victims of poverty and that lawlessness is a contagious disease." Albright has stated it neatly: "We cannot be the world's policemen, though we're very good at it."

Similar comments come from Zalmay Khalilzad, whom President Bush appointed US ambassador to the UN in 2007. He sees mutual advantages in the US-UN relationship: "The US is important for the UN. An effective US inside the UN is important for the UN, and an effective UN is important for the United States."

Exactly What Is the United Nations?

As the Preamble of the Charter declares, the world's peoples, acting through their representatives, seek to create a just and prosperous world through common action. But exactly what is the nature of this common effort? For one thing, it is *not* a form of "world government," as some may think. It is an organization of 192 sovereign nations. The world's people do not elect any of the executives who direct the organization, nor does the UN assess taxes on individuals. Furthermore, the UN can impose its will on nations only in rare and unusual circumstances, when great powers like the United States are prepared to back up the UN's actions with their own military and political might.

The UN's limitations in these regards are not always well understood in the United States. Former ambassador Richard Holbrooke tells a story about a speaking engagement in Odessa, Texas—"George Bush country," as he puts it—when "some guy asked, 'What do you think about this world government thing?' I said there was no such thing, and he said, 'What about the UN, that's a world government, they are trying to take away our liberties.' And I said, 'Well, sir, that is just not true.' There are people out there who think the UN has that kind of power and insidious influence, and the truth is the exact opposite: the UN is too weak, not too strong. You start with a certain percentage of people completely misunderstanding the UN, criticizing it from the wrong point of view. Too strong is their fear when in fact too weak to be effective is the truth."

The point about weakness is made also by analyst Jeffrey Laurenti, senior fellow at the Century Foundation, even as he emphasizes the organization's important role in shaping world opinion. He defines the organization as "a supra-political association incorporating all governments and drawing on their political authority. It is a weak membrane in terms of decision making and implementation but is nonetheless a political expression of a global sense of purpose and shared interests. The UN speaks to the aspirations of humankind. It commands public attention in most of the world as a place where world public opinion is developed and voiced and where global policy gets hammered out."

The UN System

The UN is made up of six principal organs, all based in New York except the International Court of Justice, which is based in The Hague, Netherlands:

The Secretariat

The Security Council

The General Assembly

The International Court of Justice (ICJ)

The Trusteeship Council (no longer meets)

The Economic and Social Council

—Plus UN programs and funds, which are essential to working for development, humanitarian assistance, and human rights. They include the UN Children's Fund (UNICEF), the UN Development Programme (UNDP), and the Office of the United Nations High Commissioner for Refugees (UNHCR).

—Plus the UN specialized agencies, which coordinate their work with the UN but are separate organizations. Agencies, such as the International Monetary Fund (IMF), the World Health Organization (WHO), and the International Civil Aviation Organization, focus on specific areas.

—Plus thousands of nongovernmental organizations (NGOs) that are independent citizens' organizations associated with the UN. They are concerned with many of the same issues as the UN, such as human rights, arms control, and the environment. NGOs are not part of the UN but have become important to its functioning in many key areas.

The UN's New York City headquarters is considered international territory.

Scanning the UN Flowchart

One reason the UN is often misunderstood is that few except insiders really know its structure and organizing principles. One former US ambassador to the UN in the Clinton years, Nancy Soderberg, goes so far as to claim, "There is no such single thing as the UN." Rather, the UN "is 192 countries with different agendas and a whole collection of civil servants who work there, and it's all Jell-O. You can't say what the UN is because you touch one area and it comes out looking differently on the other side." Another former US ambassador, John Bolton, adds that people have a hard time understanding the organization because "they don't know what the different pieces do, and some of the humanitarian agencies, which do work well, get lost in the shuffle."

A good beginning point for dissecting the UN is the accompanying flowchart, which lays out the basic structures and entities. At the top are the six principal organs, some of which are household names: the International Court of Justice (better known as the World Court), the Security Council (in which five selected countries have the right to veto any resolution they don't like), the General Assembly (which consists of delegates from all member nations of the UN), the Economic and Social Council (ECOSOC), the Trusteeship Council (which did its job so well it has lost its reason for being), and the Secretariat. With the exception of ECOSOC and the Trusteeship Council, these principal organs get considerable media coverage and are, in some ways, the most significant movers and shakers within the UN (see appendix A for a breakdown of UN groups).

When we move to the second tier of organizations, the scene gets more complicated. Here we find a varied collection of entities and organizations, some of which are older than the UN itself and operate with almost complete independence from it. Best known to the public are the "Specialized Agencies," such as the United Nations Educational, Scientific and Cultural Organization (UNESCO), the World Health Organization (WHO), the World Bank, and the International Monetary Fund (IMF). Another group, called "Programmes and Funds," includes one very well known body, the United Nations Chil-

The United Nations System

Principal Organs

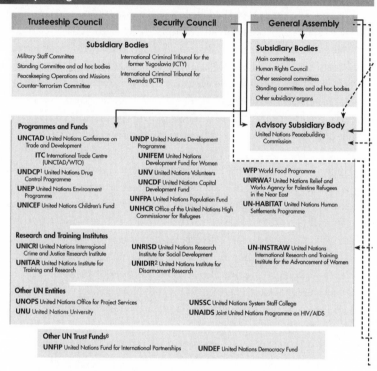

Trusteeship Council	Security Council	General Assembly

Subsidiary Bodies

Trusteeship/Security Council column:

Military Staff Committee
Standing Committee and ad hoc bodies
Peacekeeping Operations and Missions
Counter-Terrorism Committee

International Criminal Tribunal for the former Yugoslavia (ICTY)
International Criminal Tribunal for Rwanda (ICTR)

Subsidiary Bodies

Main committees
Human Rights Council
Other sessional committees
Standing committees and ad hoc bodies
Other subsidiary organs

Programmes and Funds

UNCTAD United Nations Conference on Trade and Development
　ITC International Trade Centre (UNCTAD/WTO)
UNDCP[1] United Nations Drug Control Programme
UNEP United Nations Environment Programme
UNICEF United Nations Children's Fund

UNDP United Nations Development Programme
UNIFEM United Nations Development Fund for Women
UNV United Nations Volunteers
UNCDF United Nations Capital Development Fund
UNFPA United Nations Population Fund
UNHCR Office of the United Nations High Commissioner for Refugees

Advisory Subsidiary Body

United Nations Peacebuilding Commission

WFP World Food Programme
UNRWA[2] United Nations Relief and Works Agency for Palestine Refugees in the Near East
UN-HABITAT United Nations Human Settlements Programme

Research and Training Institutes

UNICRI United Nations Interregional Crime and Justice Research Institute
UNITAR United Nations Institute for Training and Research

UNRISD United Nations Research Institute for Social Development
UNIDIR[2] United Nations Institute for Disarmament Research

UN-INSTRAW United Nations International Research and Training Institute for the Advancement of Women

Other UN Entities

UNOPS United Nations Office for Project Services
UNU United Nations University

UNSSC United Nations System Staff College
UNAIDS Joint United Nations Programme on HIV/AIDS

Other UN Trust Funds[8]

UNFIP United Nations Fund for International Partnerships
UNDEF United Nations Democracy Fund

NOTES: Solid lines from a Principal Organ indicate a direct reporting relationship; dashes indicate a non-subsidiary relationship.
[1] The UN Drug Control Programme is part of the UN Office on Drugs and Crime.
[2] UNRWA and UNIDIR report only to the GA.
[3] The United Nations Ethics Office, the United Nations Ombudsman's Office, and the Chief Information Technology Officer report directly to the Secretary-General.
[4] In an exceptional arrangement, the Under-Secretary-General for Field Support reports directly to the Under-Secretary-General for Peacekeeping Operations.
[5] IAEA reports to the Security Council and the General Assembly (GA).
[6] The CTBTO Prep.Com and OPCW report to the GA.
[7] Specialized agencies are autonomous organizations working with the UN and each other through the coordinating machinery of the ECOSOC at the intergovernmental level, and through the Chief Executives Board for coordination (CEB) at the inter-secretariat level.
[8] UNFIP is an autonomous trust fund operating under the leadership of the United Nations Deputy Secretary-General. UNDEF's advisory board recommends funding proposals for approval by the Secretary-General.

Chart of the UN Organization. UN Department of Public Information, DPI/ December 2007

Economic and Social Council

International Court of Justice

Secretariat

Functional Commissions

Commissions on:
Narcotic Drugs
Crime Prevention and Criminal Justice
Science and Technology for Development
Sustainable Development
Status of Women
Population and Development
Commission for Social Development
Statistical Commission

Regional Commissions

Economic Commission for Africa (ECA)
Economic Commission for Europe (ECE)
Economic Commission for Latin America and the Caribbean (ECLAC)
Economic and Social Commission for Asia and the Pacific (ESCAP)
Economic and Social Commission for Western Asia (ESCWA)

Other Bodies

Permanent Forum on Indigenous Issues
United Nations Forum on Forests
Sessional and standing committees
Expert, ad hoc and related bodies

Related Organizations

WTO World Trade Organization
IAEA[5] International Atomic Energy Agency

CTBTO Prep.Com[6] PrepCom for the Nuclear-Test-Ban Treaty Organization
OPCW[6] Organization for the Prohibition of Chemical Weapons

Specialized Agencies[7]

ILO International Labour Organization
FAO Food and Agriculture Organization of the United Nations
UNESCO United Nations Educational, Scientific and Cultural Organization
WHO World Health Organization

World Bank Group
   IBRD International Bank for Reconstruction and Development
   IDA International Development Association
   IFC International Finance Corporation
   MIGA Multilateral Investment Guarantee Agency
   ICSID International Centre for Settlement of Investment Disputes

IMF International Monetary Fund
ICAO International Civil Aviation Organization
IMO International Maritime Organization
ITU International Telecommunication Union
UPU Universal Postal Union
WMO World Meteorological Organization
WIPO World Intellectual Property Organization
IFAD International Fund for Agricultural Development
UNIDO United Nations Industrial Development Organization
UNWTO World Tourism Organization

Departments and Offices

OSG[3] Office of the Secretary-General
OIOS Office of Internal Oversight Services
OLA Office of Legal Affairs
DPA Department of Political Affairs
UNODA Office for Disarmament Affairs
DPKO Department of Peacekeeping Operations
DFS[4] Department of Field Support
OCHA Office for the Coordination of Humanitarian Affairs
DESA Department of Economic and Social Affairs
DGACM Department for General Assembly and Conference Management
DPI Department of Public Information
DM Department of Management
UN-OHRLLS Office of the High Representative for the Least Developed Countries, Landlocked Developing Countries and Small Island Developing States
OHCHR Office of the United Nations High Commissioner for Human Rights
UNODC United Nations Office on Drugs and Crime
DSS Department of Safety and Security

ⓒⓢⓡⓞ

UNOG UN Office at Geneva
UNOV UN Office at Vienna
UNON UN Office at Nairobi

Published by the United Nations
Department of Public Information
DPI/2470—07-49950—December 2007—3M

What It Means to You

"I know that the UN often frustrates Americans, and I am acutely aware of its shortcomings. But that is precisely why the United States must carry out sustained, concerted, and strategic multilateral diplomacy. Many countries invest heavily in deliberations on what they view as the 'world stage.' That in part explains why diplomacy at the UN can be slow, frustrating, complex, and imperfect. But that is also why effective American diplomacy at the United Nations remains so crucial."   —Susan E. Rice, US ambassador to the UN

dren's Fund (UNICEF), and several others that appear frequently in the news, like the United Nations Environment Programme (which monitors climate change and other environmental issues) and the United Nations High Commissioner for Refugees (UNHCR). Below them on the chart are "Other UN Entities," featuring one standout, the Human Rights Council, which meets in Geneva and receives heavy press coverage, and three others that play important but less publicized roles. The five research institutes likewise keep a low public profile.

The "Related Organizations" contain such entities as the World Trade Organization, the International Atomic Energy Agency (IAEA), and two sets of commissions. The "Functional Commissions" include some that on first glance seem to poach on the ground of other entities. For example, the Commission on Narcotic Drugs seems to overlap the UN Drug Control Programme, on the left side of the chart. Similarly, the Commission on the Status of Women seems to overlap the UN Development Fund for Women. However, the overlap is more apparent than real in these two cases, because the Functional Commissions concentrate on policy, while the agencies are oriented more toward implementation. In addition we find the "Regional Commissions," which are among the least known of UN bodies. They set policy about economic development in the regions of Africa, Europe, Latin America and the Caribbean, Asia and the Pacific, and Western Asia.

Two Ends of the Telescope

"I think that now being in national government, it again reaffirms for me the extraordinary possibility of the United Nations, in that so many problems that land on my desk, if we are to move them forward in a way that benefits UK national interests, the place to go is the UN because for all sorts of reasons [the problems] are not amenable to a bilateral solution. This multilateralization of the foreign policy agenda is a real phenomenon that I see where I'm sitting now, as clearly from this end of the telescope as when I was at the other end.

"The other thing that I see very clearly is the challenge of the UN to live up to that opportunity. There's a sense when you are a national government, that when you push something over to the UN for solution, you're likely to be subjecting it to delays and compromises and confusion, and process is going to triumph over substance and results. In sum, I see as clearly from the national end as I did from the UN end the opportunity, but I equally see the problem of capacity and robustness in terms of the UN finding solutions to problems."
—Mark Malloch Brown, former deputy-secretary-general of the UN

How It Works

We now have a good schematic picture of the UN's structure. But this is only a beginning. When we think about these organizations in action, flowcharts aren't very helpful because they don't show how the parts interact or how effective or efficient they are. They don't show, for example, that regional blocs control most of the votes in the main deliberative body, the General Assembly. The blocs are invisible yet powerful actors on the UN stage. The flowchart also does not explain that although the "supporting organizations" sit below specific other organizations, they are not merely adjuncts of those organizations. On the contrary, many of the supporting organizations run their own affairs with little interference and, as critics have complained, with not much communication with the peer agencies, programs, or commissions with which they share interests.

Worth Fixing

"The UN continues to be vital to the functioning of the international system, but it needs reform. It needs a lot of support by nations. It needs to really keep revitalizing itself. I am a great believer in the UN, but there have to be some very serious reforms."
—Madeleine Albright, former US ambassador to the UN

The fact that the UN is overseen by 192 member states, often with varying agendas, can contribute to a degree of administrative waffling and diplomatic theatrics. Brian Urquhart, who participated in creating the UN, argues, however, that the shortcomings have to be balanced against the strengths. "There's quiet diplomacy, which goes on twenty-four hours a day," he says. "There's the secretary-general and the Secretariat, who, contrary to general belief, are rather effective and not, incidentally, a great bloated organization. . . . The UN is not very efficient, I have to say, in some respects, because it's recruited from all over the world, and you have to work hard to get a common standard going, but it does work." He concludes, "The UN is like an insurance policy: you hate paying for it, but it's useful if something goes wrong."

Secretary-General Ban Ki-moon emphasizes the unique position of the UN as an honest broker. "At the United Nations we have great convening power to find global solutions to our global problems." And problems there surely are, from terrorism and nuclear proliferation to worldwide hunger and disease, "to name just a few." These threats "cannot be approached," says the secretary-general, "as items on a list. The trick is to see them as part of a broader whole. In truth, solutions to one are solutions to all. The key is to see the interconnections among all the problems that come to our door at the UN."

What's in It for Us?

Putting aside international diplomacy, why should Americans care about the UN? Pressed to identify a specific UN-related item or service

The UN and the Nobel Peace Prize

The Nobel Peace Prize has been awarded on ten occasions to the UN, its specialized agencies, and staff. The UN High Commissioner for Refugees has twice received the prize.

2007   Intergovernmental Panel on Climate Change and Al Gore, Jr.
2005   International Atomic Energy Agency and Mohammed ElBaradei
2001   United Nations and Kofi Annan
1988   United Nations Peacekeeping Forces
1981   Office of the UN High Commissioner for Refugees
1969   International Labour Organization
1965   United Nations Children's Fund
1961   Dag Hammarskjöld
1954   Office of the UN High Commissioner for Refugees
1950   Ralph Bunche

they have encountered recently, people might mention UNICEF trick-or-treat boxes and holiday cards. But is that all? The UN sets standards that affect us every day. "You may think that you have never benefited personally from the UN," says Madeleine Albright, "but if you have ever traveled on an international airline or shipping line or placed a phone call overseas or received mail from outside the country or been thankful for an accurate weather report—then you have been served directly or indirectly by one part or another of the UN system." For a global power like the United States, says Zalmay Khalilzad, the world body is a very important instrument that should be made as effective as possible and "reformed as we go forward so that it can maintain the confidence of people and countries around the world." Susan Rice, who became UN ambassador under President Obama, warns that the UN "is not a cure-all; we must be clear-eyed about the problems, challenges, and frustrations of the institution." But, she continues, it is also "a global institution that can address a tremendous range of critical American and global interests."

CHAPTER 2

Founding Documents

[The UN is] immensely important because it represents legitimacy and international law, without which we'll all eventually go into the ditch. It represents a place where in emergencies you can actually do something . . . that will be accepted even by people . . . who would not accept an intervention by the US or any other single country.

—Brian Urquhart, aide and adviser to UN
secretaries-general, 1946–86

As with any organization that exists in this ever-changing world, the UN cannot act according to an unchanging set of rules. It possesses two documents to guide its members. The first is the UN Charter, written in 1945, which functions as the Constitution does for the United States and, like the Constitution, has been amended over time to reflect changing needs. The second is the Universal Declaration of Human Rights, which is a manifesto of human dignity and value that remains as fresh and radical now as it was when adopted in 1948 (the Declaration is printed in appendix B).

The Charter

The Charter was signed on June 26, 1945, by fifty nations and entered into force several months later, on October 24. The chapters and articles constitute a treaty and are legally binding on the signatories. Article 103 of the Charter stipulates that if a member state finds that its obligations under the Charter conflict with duties under "any other international agreement," the state must place its Charter obligations first.

Nineteen chapters lay out the major components of the organization, including its director (the secretary-general), its lines of authority, and the responsibilities and rights of its members—that is, of governments that constitute the UN membership. Chapter I describes the purpose of the UN, emphasizing international peace and security, and Chapter II lists the qualifications for membership. Most of the information about the elements of the new organization, including its six principal organs, appears in Chapters III through XV. Chapter XIX describes the process for amending the Charter, something that has rarely been done. One change, in 1965, enlarged the Security Council from eleven to fifteen members; two other changes concerned enlarging the Economic and Social Council.

The Charter clearly envisions the members as sovereign and independent states (Chapter I, Article 2) and requires that they resolve their disputes with one another without endangering international peace and security (Article 3). Member states are also asked to avoid threatening other nations with the use of force (Article 4) and to assist the UN with any actions it may take (Article 5). The final article of Chapter I attempts to balance the internal affairs of each member state with its international actions and responsibilities. It states that the UN is not authorized to intervene in domestic affairs of a member state, but it also says that this restriction does not limit the right of the UN under Chapter VII. That chapter gives the Security Council the authority to resolve international disputes through negotiation, economic, military, and other sanctions, and even the use of force.

Franklin Roosevelt died in April 1945, leaving it to others to realize

The UN Charter is signed at the San Francisco conference, June 26, 1945.
UN Photo

The Charter and National Sovereignty

"Sovereign entities have created a supra-association in which they have invested a small measure of sovereignty, at least for the purpose of preventing war. The UN Charter represents very small concessions of sovereignty to the global entity, the UN, but it was primarily to prevent a return to war."   —Jeffrey Laurenti, Century Foundation his dream of a United Nations. Roosevelt's widow, Eleanor, had gained a reputation as a champion of the poor and disenfranchised, and President Harry Truman now appointed her to the distinguished list of delegates to the first meeting of the General Assembly in London, in 1945. There she served as the sole female member of Committee III, slated to address humanitarian, social, and cultural matters.

The Universal Declaration of Human Rights

After her impressive performance in London, the White House and the State Department felt comfortable asking Eleanor Roosevelt to represent the government on the nascent UN Human Rights Commission and to help draft what was to become the Universal Declaration of Human Rights. Many experts at the time believed that the League of Nations had been fatally flawed because its charter lacked a strong statement in favor of human rights. Many supporters of the UN had originally hoped to launch the new organization with both a charter and a declaration of human rights. "I felt extremely strongly that human rights were something which simply had to be developed into an international rule," recalls Brian Urquhart, who participated in the commission's proceedings. "It simply wasn't good enough to try to rely on people to behave reasonably well: they don't. The Nazis were an extreme, but they are not unique."

The new Human Rights Commission, with Eleanor Roosevelt as its chair, began meeting to write the declaration in April 1946. It kept meeting for the next two and a half years, in New York City and then Geneva, Switzerland, until it finally hammered out a consensus document. Many difficulties arose as the eighteen delegates, who represented a wide spectrum of political, social, cultural, and religious views, discussed and debated the nature of rights—indeed, the meaning of being a human being—and the proper relation between the individual and the state.

An unexpected debate arose over the use of the noun "man" to stand for "humankind" in the very first article of the draft. The original text read, "All men are created equal." Hansa Mehta of India, a

Eleanor Roosevelt with the Universal Declaration of Human Rights, November 1949. UN Photo

woman, complained that the word could be misunderstood to exclude women. The UN's Commission on the Status of Women voted unanimously to ask the Commission on Human Rights to substitute "all people" for "all men." Eleanor Roosevelt was divided on the issue because she had never felt excluded by the use of "man" in the Declaration of Independence. But she relented, and the phrase "all human beings" became the definitive term in the draft.

When the Universal Declaration was finished, it was sent to the General Assembly, which debated it anew. Finally, at 3:00 am on December 10, 1948, the General Assembly voted to adopt the draft.

Resting on Enlightenment ideals of human dignity, the Universal Declaration is unique both in its breadth and in its success as an international standard by which to identify the basic rights that every person should enjoy. Most human rights laws, and many national constitutions, reflect its provisions. It is an inspiration to people seeking freedom and to organizations advancing the cause of freedom and justice. Brian Urquhart praises the Universal Declaration "as one of the most important actions in the twentieth century because it changed the perception of human society from being a society where governments were dominant to a society where individual rights were the thing that everybody, including governments, had to worry about."

Unlike the Charter, the Universal Declaration is not a treaty, and its provisions therefore are not law, but the declaration has been largely incorporated into two international treaties that came into effect in 1976 and have been accepted by most member states: the International Covenant on Economic, Social, and Cultural Rights and the International Covenant on Civil and Political Rights. The UN refers to these covenants and the Universal Declaration as the International Bill of Rights.

CHAPTER 3

The Secretary-General and the Secretariat

I believe in the power of relationships. For years I have carried in my wallet . . . a well-worn scrap of paper inscribed with Chinese characters pertaining to one's age and phase in life. At 30, you are in your prime of life. At 50, you are said to know your destiny. At 60, you possess the wisdom of the "soft ear."   —Ban Ki-moon, secretary-general of the UN

On October 13, 2006, the United Nations General Assembly selected a sixty-one-year-old South Korean, Ban Ki-moon, as the eighth secretary-general, to succeed Kofi Annan, whose two five-year terms had set precedents for international activism and public visibility. The new man attracted wide media attention. The secretary-general is sometimes referred to as the world's secular pope and carries heavy responsibilities in such vital and sensitive areas as peacemaking, human rights, and UN reform. Yet outside the diplomatic community, few had heard of Ban Ki-moon. No wonder people around the globe were asking, Who is this fellow?

Ban Ki-moon was born in a South Korean farming village in 1944 and grew up when his country was defending itself against aggression from the north—a war fought under US leadership with the official

Ban Ki-moon as secretary-general-designate in front of UN headquarters.
UN Photo/Eskinder Debebe

sanction of the UN. The young man's life took a decisive turn when he won a high school essay contest sponsored by the Red Cross that led to a visit to the United States. He credits a brief meeting with President John F. Kennedy in Washington, DC, with helping him decide to pursue a career in diplomacy. Back in South Korea, Ban joined the Ministry of Foreign Affairs in 1970 and gradually moved up the career ladder, earning respect for his intense work ethic and his diplomatic skills. In 1974 he was posted to New York City as first secretary of the

South Korean Permanent Observer Mission to the UN, and in 1991 he became director of the foreign ministry's United Nations Division. Meanwhile, in 1980, he became director of the International Organizations and Treaties Bureau, in Seoul. After two postings to the Korean embassy in Washington, DC, and more assignments in Korea and Austria, he became his country's foreign minister in 2004. By then he had also earned a master's degree in public administration at Harvard University's prestigious Kennedy School of Government.

Choosing the Secretary-General

Ban declared his candidacy for secretary-general of the UN in February 2006 and launched a vigorous campaign for the position with strong support from his home government. Ban Ki-moon's efforts got a huge boost when it became known that both China and the United States favored his candidacy. His chances were also aided by the unwritten agreement that the post of secretary-general should rotate among regions of the world. Accordingly, Javier Pérez de Cuéllar, from Peru, served two terms (1982–91) and was followed by Boutros Boutros-Ghali, of Egypt, who served one term (1992–97), and Kofi Annan, a Ghanaian, who served two terms (1997–2006). Because Africa had contributed two consecutive secretaries-general, and Europe had produced several secretaries-general, ending with Kurt Waldheim (1972–81) of Austria, the post was due to go next to Asia (which, in the UN system, includes the Arab states of the Middle East). Ban Ki-moon was therefore qualified to run for the office, but he faced serious competition from another Asian candidate, Shashi Tharoor of India, an experienced UN staffer closely associated with Kofi Annan.

Once Ban and Tharoor had declared, the UN began the formal process of deciding on a winner. The procedure involves two UN bodies: the Security Council, which recommends a candidate, and the General Assembly, which ratifies the choice. The Security Council decides on the nomination at "private" meetings that have no public record except for brief communiqués from its president. In 2006, the fifteen members of the council held a series of straw polls that made

Secretaries-general

Trygve Lie (Norway)	1945–52
Dag Hammarskjöld (Sweden)	1953–61
U Thant (Burma)	1961–71
Kurt Waldheim (Austria)	1972–81
Javier Pérez de Cuellar (Peru)	1982–91
Boutros Boutros-Ghali (Egypt)	1992–97
Kofi Annan (Ghana)	1997–2006
Ban Ki-moon (South Korea)	2007–present

Ban Ki-moon the favorite, with Tharoor second. Observers did note a surprisingly strong showing by Vaira Vike-Freiberga of Latvia, the only woman and non-Asian among the candidates, whose name was placed in two straw votes. When the final poll showed Ban Ki-moon as the nominee, the council passed his name to the General Assembly, and in the ensuing vote Ban was elected the eighth secretary-general.

An Evolving Job Description

The position of the secretary-general, only briefly described in the UN Charter, has evolved over time. "In the Charter of the UN," says Richard Holbrooke, "the role of secretary-general is only described with a single phrase, that the UN will have a chief administrative officer. It doesn't describe the authority of the secretary-general as the Constitution describes the powers for the president and Congress. It's all been done, like the British constitution, by precedent and strong secretaries-general, of whom we've had two, Dag Hammarskjöld and Kofi Annan."

Mark Malloch Brown adds that the Charter "doesn't envisage significant powers for the secretary-general in international relations." Rather, he says, the internationally active secretaries-general have succeeded by "convincing genuinely important individuals, heads of government and so on, that they can be helpful." Michael Sheehan, a

Secretary-General Dag Hammarskjöld on a peace mission in Congo, 1961. UN Photo

From the UN Charter, Chapter XV

ARTICLE 97

The Secretariat shall comprise a Secretary-General and such staff as the Organization may require. The Secretary-General shall be appointed by the General Assembly upon the recommendation of the Security Council. He shall be the chief administrative officer of the Organization.

former assistant secretary-general for peacekeeping, says that one of the secretary-general's roles is to "tell the Security Council what it has to know, not what it wants to hear. So the Secretariat is not just a puppet on a string of the member states; it has a role, and there's a dialogue between the Secretariat and the member states."

The many, often conflicting responsibilities of the secretary-general make the post one of the most demanding imaginable. It requires

Secretary-General Ban Ki-moon confers with former secretary-general Kofi Annan, March 4, 2008. UN Photo/Mark Garten

intelligence and experience, certainly, but also drive, vision, and infinite tact and patience. The secretary-general must be able to communicate with the entire UN family as well as with all the nations of the world while administering a global array of programs and agencies.

The Secretariat

The secretary-general conducts operations through the Secretariat, which is a kind of international bureau consisting of approximately nine thousand staff members from about 160 countries. Most of them work in the New York City headquarters, but the Secretariat has other offices in Geneva, Vienna, and Nairobi. In keeping with the letter and spirit of the Charter, which aimed to create an international civil service, member states agree not to exert improper influence on the Secretariat's staff, and the staff, in turn, take an oath that they will be responsible solely to the United Nations and will not seek or take directions from any other authority. Nancy Soderberg rates the Secretariat as "a collection of really dynamic individuals who care deeply about the organization and really work their tails off, interspersed with incompetent people who are there for regional balance, who are just never going to get fired."

Other insiders rate the staff's quality as more mixed, with a few outstanding people, many good ones, and quite a few careerists who simply put in a day's work. Former Canadian ambassador David Malone estimates that "40 percent of the Secretariat staff are movers and shakers and carry the full burden of action. About 30 percent do no harm and do no good, and about 30 percent spend their time making trouble. Which means that the 40 percent who get work done are fairly heroic, and they exist at all levels of the system." When assessing the quality of the personnel, it is important to understand that senior UN appointments must be approved by a majority of the General Assembly's members.

Kofi Annan is credited with advancing a series of administrative reforms (discussed in chapter 14) begun by his predecessor, Boutros Boutros-Ghali. He encouraged development of a corporate culture aimed at making results, not efforts, the test of effectiveness. An upshot was the creation of a new post, deputy secretary-general of the UN, established in 1997 to help manage the Secretariat and coordinate UN programs and activities, especially those relating to economic and social development.

The deputy secretary-general assists the secretary-general and represents the UN at conferences and official functions. She or he chairs the Steering Committee on Reform and Management Policy and the Advisory Board of the UN Fund for International Partnerships (UNFIP), which handles relations with the foundation set up by media mogul Ted Turner in support of the UN (see chapter 16).

Annan named a Canadian diplomat, Louise Fréchette, to the new position in 1998. She was succeeded by Mark Malloch Brown, appointed by Kofi Annan in 2006. In 2007, Ban Ki-moon selected lawyer and former foreign minister of Tanzania Asha-Rose Migiro to the post.

A New Agenda

As secretary-general, Ban Ki-moon carries a much lower profile than his charismatic predecessor. Kofi Annan was an activist secretary-general who stretched his office to fit an expanded vision of international diplomacy and action. Annan received glowing reviews during his first term, only to find his image tarnished by affairs like the Oil-for-Food scandal during his second. Nevertheless, many insiders and experts still regard him as one of the best secretary-generals ever appointed. As Mark Malloch Brown put it in an interview several years ago, "We've had a series of secretaries-general since Hammarskjöld who were more secretaries than generals. This is the first time since then we have a secretary-general who dwarfs his institution." William Luers, president of the United Nations Association of the United States (UNAUSA), describes Annan as the "conscience of the world" and "a global spokesman, a credible voice for the international community at a time when none were competing with him. When he left, the UN had become a center of international activity it rarely had in its history. During his ten years, the growth of UN global responsibility was almost unmatched."

Ban has been careful to promise only what he thinks he can deliver. Luers rates him "a better talker than orator. He likes one on one and conversational exchanges. He sets priorities and doesn't try to do too much. He is an extremely hard worker and very focused on core problems." Former UN ambassador John Bolton approves Ban's more measured approach, in contrast to that of Annan, whose "ambitions were too sweeping." "I do think there is very broad agreement that [Ban's] low-key style of management is widely approved by all different parts of the world. In that sense he has cooled things off in New York, and there's general agreement it was less offensive." Indeed, Ban skillfully used his links with two of his most powerful backers to advance extremely difficult negotiations on both Darfur

Secretary-General Ban Ki-moon and his wife visit a primary school in Burkino Faso, April 23, 2008. UN Photo/Eskinder Debebe

Deeds More Than Words

Secretary-General Ban Ki-moon has "modesty of pretense and modesty of promises," but not "modesty of ambition and delivery." Rather, he is "proving to be a blue-collar secretary-general, rolling up his sleeves and being devoted and resilient but not making headlines and serious mistakes."
—Edward Luck, International Peace Institute

(opposed by China) and climate change (opposed by both China and the United States).

Ban Ki-moon has clearly stated his agenda, and it begins with basics: Protect the global climate because otherwise we are all threatened. Intervene when nations or regions fall into chaos and destruc-

From the UN Charter, Chapter XV

ARTICLE 99

The Secretary-General may bring to the attention of the Security Council any matter which in his opinion may threaten the maintenance of international peace and security.

ARTICLE 100

1. In the performance of their duties the Secretary-General and the staff shall not seek or receive instructions from any government or from any other authority external to the Organization. They shall refrain from any action which might reflect on their position as international officials responsible only to the Organization.
2. Each Member of the United Nations undertakes to respect the exclusively international character of the responsibilities of the Secretary-General and the staff and not to seek to influence them in the discharge of their responsibilities.

ARTICLE 101

1. The staff shall be appointed by the Secretary-General under regulations established by the General Assembly.
2. Appropriate staffs shall be permanently assigned to the Economic and Social Council, the Trusteeship Council, and, as required, to other organs of the United Nations. These staffs shall form a part of the Secretariat.
3. The paramount consideration in the employment of the staff and in the determination of the conditions of service shall be the necessity of securing the highest standards of efficiency, competence, and integrity. Due regard shall be paid to the importance of recruiting the staff on as wide a geographical basis as possible.

Secretary-General-designate Ban Ki-Moon and former US secretary of state
Madeleine Albright, November 17, 2006. UN/Mark Garten

tion because it is our human duty to do so. Stop nuclear proliferation
because it could lead, among other evils, to terrorist groups gaining
possession of weapons of mass destruction. Fulfill the eight Millennium Development Goals (discussed in chapter 15), which are intended to bring the poorest nations to an acceptable level of social and
economic development. And reform the UN's fiscal and management
structure to make it more efficient and give it the means to address an
escalating series of needs and demands from the world community.

No one person or office can tackle this agenda alone, of course. The
secretary-general is but the most visible official among many in the
UN, and the Secretariat is one among many entities both within and
outside of the UN. It's time to take a closer look at these people and
organizations, beginning with the secretary-general's most important
working partner.

CHAPTER 4

The American Ambassador

Permanent representatives [of the United States] have to spend a lot of time in Washington, and that's what's distinctive. Part of their influence and power at the UN is directly linked to peoples' perceptions of their clout in Washington. So when the permanent rep can't make a meeting because he or she has to be in Washington, that is seen as a sign of clout.
—Jeffrey Laurenti, senior fellow at the Century Foundation

Each of the 192 member nations maintains a UN mission in New York City, staffed by a head, known as the permanent representative, who also carries the title of ambassador. The term of the permanent representative varies by nation, usually extending over several years. So the word "permanent" shouldn't be taken too literally, but it conveniently denotes the key person in a delegation of representatives.

The US permanent representative has the highest-visibility job at the United Nations, next to the secretary-general, and one of the most complicated owing to US geopolitical eminence and the Byzantine nature of US policy-making. "The job of an American ambassador at the UN is particularly tough," says former Canadian ambassador David Malone. "Most ambassadors at the UN get one set of instruc-

US Permanent Representatives to the UN, 1946–2007

Edward R. Stettinius Jr. (March 1946–June 1946)

Herschel V. Johnson (acting) (June 1946–January 1947)

Warren R. Austin (January 1947–January 1953)

Henry Cabot Lodge Jr. (January 1953–September 1960)

James J. Wadsworth (September 1960–January 1961)

Adlai E. Stevenson (January 1961–July 1965)

Arthur J. Goldberg (July 1965–June 1968)

George W. Ball (June 1968–September 1968)

James Russell Wiggins (October 1968–January 1969)

Charles W. Yost (January 1969–February 1971)

George H. W. Bush (February 1971–January 1973)

John P. Scali (February 1973–June 1975)

Daniel P. Moynihan (June 1975–February 1976)

William W. Scranton (March 1976–January 1977)

Andrew Young (January 1977–April 1979)

Donald McHenry (April 1979–January 1981)

Jeane J. Kirkpatrick (February 1981–April 1985)

Vernon A. Walters (May 1985–January 1989)

Thomas R. Pickering (March 1989–May 1992)

Edward J. Perkins (May 1992–January 1993)

Madeleine K. Albright (February 1993–January 1997)

Bill Richardson (February 1997–September 1998)

Peter Burleigh, Chargé d'Affaires (September 1998–August 1999)

Richard C. Holbrooke (August 1999–January 2001)

John D. Negroponte (September 2001–June 2004)

John C. Danforth (June 2004–January 2005)

John R. Bolton (August 2005–December 2006)

Zalmay M. Khalilzad (April 2007–2008)

Susan E. Rice (2009–present)

tions that are channeled through the foreign minister, and occasionally they will hear from their head of government or head of state. In the US system, the ambassador's influence depends on whether the president gives the post cabinet rank, as Clinton and Obama did, or places it under the direct authority of the secretary of state, as George W. Bush did.

Consummate diplomatic skill is required to manage such a complicated chain of command while still accomplishing desired goals at the UN. "To influence developments, you have to work with the secretary-general and the Secretariat," comments former UN ambassador Zalmay Khalilzad about his approach to diplomacy, "but you also need to convince sufficient UN members to have decisions made." Compared with Afghanistan and Iraq, which were his previous ambassadorial postings, "it's a very different assignment" because "you are not coming to a sovereign entity, and the secretary-general is not a president or a prime minister." Khalilzad was also mindful of his base in Washington. He saw himself as "the bridge between the administration and the UN headquarters," explaining "both the opportunities and the challenges that the UN presents to people in Washington."

David Malone suggests that when Madeleine Albright was permanent representative she had "real influence" in Washington but preferred not to take too many risks because she was hoping for an even bigger job, which she got when she became secretary of state. She practiced "endless diplomacy," Malone claims, not so much in New York as in Washington, "in order not to make enemies." Richard Holbrooke felt sufficiently strong in Washington to define a "Holbrooke policy" at the UN and to expect others to follow it. Amazingly, says Malone, they generally did. "Nobody really spoke back to him. He had the ear of the president. The vice president liked and respected him. . . . He essentially made policy on every subject that he discussed at the UN, and he then advised Washington on what their policy was henceforth to be. It was a very interesting performance."

Few permanent representatives have assumed office under more difficult conditions than John Negroponte, appointed by President George W. Bush, who was sworn in as US representative to the UN on

Former US ambassador to the UN Richard Holbrooke meets with Secretary-General Ban Ki-Moon, November 30, 2007. UN Photo/Eskinder Debebe

September 18, 2001, only one week after 9/11. "I arrived here the nineteenth of September," he noted in an interview given shortly after his appointment, "and my experience has been very much shaped by the events of September 11 and our response to that."

Negroponte needed all his diplomatic skills as US permanent representative, although he used them very differently than in his previous posts. In some of his former diplomatic assignments, such as ambassador to Mexico and to the Philippines, he had time to become an expert on each nation and culture, but at the UN he had to deal with an endless variety of people and issues. "To be a representative here, you have to know a little bit about a lot of issues. And managing your own time so you make sure you know what you need to know in order to be effective is a challenge because some days on your agenda there are three or four various conflicts that come up."

Negroponte also became familiar with the UN penchant for debates

President-elect Barack Obama introduces Senator Hillary Clinton as his
choice for secretary of state and Susan Rice as UN ambassador, December 1,
2008. Scott Olson/Getty Images

and resolutions, especially relating to Israel and the Palestinians. "I've
been a little bit distressed by how much time does get absorbed on what
I consider to be a pretty sterile Middle Eastern debate," he stated. Acknowledging that some discussion about the Middle East has been constructive—particularly one resolution, 1397, that affirmed the vision of
a Palestinian state, which the US mission initiated—he nevertheless
concluded that "the protagonists see the UN as a forum, just another
public arena, rather than a way of really devising solutions to problems."

Negroponte often found that his hardest job was managing the
home base. In New York the UN has great public visibility and strong
political support. "There is a natural constituency," said Negroponte.
"But outside of New York and outside the Beltway, that's more of a
challenge." After Negroponte left the UN to become ambassador to

Restoring US Leadership

"There is no country more capable than the United States to exercise leadership in this global institution, and to help frame its programs and shape its actions. My most immediate objective . . . will be to refresh and renew America's leadership in the United Nations and bring to bear the full weight of our influence, voice, resources, values, and diplomacy at the United Nations."
—Susan E. Rice, US ambassador to the UN

Iraq in 2004, John C. Danforth became permanent representative. A lawyer and former politician with foreign affairs experience, Danforth spent eighteen years as a Republican senator from Missouri before re-tiring—he thought—from full-time public life. After Danforth's depar-ture in early 2005, the White House made a controversial appointment in John Bolton, who was perceived by some in and out of Congress as unfriendly to the UN. Indeed, Congress refused to approve Bolton's appointment, and the new permanent representative served in what was effectively an interim position before resigning at the end of 2006.

Bolton was succeeded by Zalmay Khalilzad, an experienced diplo-mat whose style offered a sharp contrast to Bolton's lawyerly assertive-ness and blunt approach. Khalilzad's more traditional diplomatic style helped gained him a reputation for thoughtful attentiveness. Long-time UN insider Mark Malloch Brown recalls having coffee with Khal-ilzad in September 2007 in the General Assembly's delegates lounge, "and even the coffeemaker considered himself Zal Khalilzad's best friend." Says Malloch Brown, "he's congenial, he's approachable, he listens, and he argues back to Washington about what the UN per-spective is on issues and how Washington can therefore better attain its objectives."

When Barack Obama was elected president in 2008, he promptly nominated a close adviser, Susan E. Rice, as the new UN ambassador. Educated at Stanford University and later Oxford, Rice quickly gained a reputation for toughness. "If I were to characterize her," remarked her friend Madeleine Albright, "whether it's playing basketball or anything else, she's fearless." Rice served as UN specialist on the Clinton National Security Council staff and then became an assistant secretary of state for Africa. During those years she witnessed the aftermath of the Rwanda genocide, including fields strewn with mutilated corpses, and there resolved that the world must never allow such acts to occur again. UN insiders note approvingly that Rice's appointment carries cabinet rank, which signals a close working relationship with the president.

Many of the US permanent representatives have cited the office's high-profile nature as giving it a quality all its own. John Danforth remarked that the difference came home to him, quite literally, only a few days after he assumed his post in New York, when he opened the morning newspaper and saw a front-page story presenting his comments at the UN the previous day as "the US says. . . ." Turning to his wife, he quipped, "That's me. I am the United States when I speak." He found it "a very sobering moment."

CHAPTER 5

The Security Council

In order to ensure prompt and effective action by the United Nations, its Members confer on the Security Council primary responsibility for the maintenance of international peace and security, and agree that in carrying out its duties under this responsibility the Security Council acts on their behalf.
—UN Charter

The Security Council is the United Nations' enforcer, charged with making the world a safer, more stable place by preventing or stopping armed conflict among and even within nations. The council is the only UN principal organ whose resolutions are binding on member states. It has the authority to examine any conflict or dispute that might have international repercussions. It can identify aggressive action by states and call on UN members to make an appropriate response, including application of economic sanctions and even military action. The Security Council has the authority to decide matters affecting the fate of governments, establish peacekeeping missions, create tribunals to try persons accused of war crimes, and in extreme cases declare a nation to be fair game for corrective action by other member states.

The council's preeminent authority has made it increasingly popular as the prime center of activity whenever a major international crisis erupts. After the Cold War, when East-West relations began to thaw, the council became much more active and more willing to extend its reach. The number of its formal meetings and informal consultations grew from 117 in 1988 to 321 by 1992 and 532 in 2002.

A Hands-On Council

Over that time span the Security Council has evolved—a point stressed by Edward Luck of Columbia University and the International Peace Institute. An expert about the council, he remarks that "people forget how the council has changed over the years. Some say it is archaic, created in 1945, but if you look at its working methods since the mid-1990s, it has changed. It's more open." The council is much more likely, nowadays, to invite nonmembers to speak before it and to ask advice from UN officials and agencies. Council members now sometimes make on-site visits to peacekeeping missions or other UN operations. In 2007, for example, council members visited Belgrade and Kosovo to see the situation on the ground for themselves, and in summer 2008 they made a fact-funding tour of Africa, including Sudan's Darfur region. The council has also accumulated nearly thirty so-called subsidiary bodies, such as the Counter-Terrorism Committee. "It is an interactive council," claims Luck. "It doesn't just sit on Mount Olympus."

The Security Council's greater activity has reinforced its profile as a factor in global affairs. When the United States and its allies decided to invade Iraq in 2003 and topple the Saddam Hussein regime, the Bush administration tried strenuously to gain the council's backing for invasion. After the war, the US government worked hard to mend its fences with the UN and encourage the world body to become more closely involved in the shattered country's reconstruction and reconciliation. According to Edward Luck, "People throughout much of the world" have come to accept that the council's authorization is "either mandatory or highly preferable prior to the use of force." Luck sees

US Ambassador Zalmay Khalilzad addresses the Security Council on the
Middle East, January 22, 2008. UN Photo/Evan Schneider

that as a significant development: "Hardheaded realists should take
note, for something is changing in terms of international norms and
public perceptions regarding the rules of warfare, the use of force, and
sources of legitimacy."

P5 and E10

The Security Council consists of fifteen members. Five—the Permanent Five, or P5, hold their seats by authority of the Charter—China,
France, the Russian Federation, the United Kingdom, and the United
States. The other ten, the so-called E10, are elected by the General
Assembly to two-year terms. The council is presided over by the president, an office that rotates monthly, according to the English alpha-
betical listing of council member states.

The Permanent Five carry special weight in the council, in part
because of their permanent status and their importance as large, pow-

Table I. Security Council Meetings, Resolutions, and Vetoes, 1996–2007

Year	Meetings	Resolutions Considered	Resolutions Adopted	US Vetoes	Chinese Vetoes	Russian Vetoes
2007	202	57	56	0	1	1
2006	273	89	87	2	0	0
2005	235	71	71	0	0	0
2004	216	62	59	2	0	1
2003	208	69	67	2	0	0
2002	238	70	68	2	0	0
2001	192	54	52	2	0	0
2000	167	52	50	0	0	0
1999	124	67	65	0	1	0
1998	116	73	73	0	0	0
1997	117	57	54	2	1	0
1996	114	59	57	1	0	0

Source: Adapted from US Department of State, *Twenty-fifth Annual Report on Voting Practices in the UN, 2007*, 13; and Global Policy Forum, "Changing Patterns in the Use of the Veto in the Security Council," www.globalpolicy .org/security/data/vetotab.htm

erful nations and in part because each holds a trump card in the form of a veto. When a P5 member votes no on a resolution, that kills it, even if the other fourteen council members vote yes. A permanent member can abstain from voting if it does not want to take a public stand on a measure. If it objects to a measure but cannot find the votes to defeat it, it can exercise the veto. The veto was more common when the world was divided into communist and noncommunist blocs, but in recent years it has become rare (see table 1). In 2007, for example, the only vetoes were by China and Russia in objection to a measure about Myanmar (Burma).

One result of the council's prestige is that being elected to it is highly coveted by the UN's member states, which campaign in the General Assembly for the honor. Each E10 member serves a two-year term, and candidacies are apportioned through a quota system that

Source of Legitimacy

The Security Council is "the most important international body in the world. Countries give it legitimacy because it can authorize the use of force for peacemaking or even a war, as in Korea, Kuwait, and Afghanistan."   —Richard Holbrooke, former US ambassador to the UN

Sixth Veto

The E10 have leverage in the Security Council, not through veto power, but through their voting majority. Because it takes nine votes to pass a resolution, it is possible for the E10 to block passage if they vote as a bloc. This voting leverage is sometimes referred to as the "sixth veto."

the General Assembly has devised based on regions: three seats for Africa, two for Latin America, one for Asia, one for Arab nations, one for Eastern Europe, and two for Western Europe. Sometimes a seat is uncontested because the regional member states have agreed on who should hold it. The African Group, for example, rotates candidates based on subregions—Southern Africa, Central Africa, East Africa, North Africa, and West Africa—so that eventually every African nation will have the opportunity to serve for a two-year term. The other groups, by contrast, have no fixed practice on nominations.

The P5 Club

Acting as a sort of club, the Permanent Five usually play a leading role in deliberations. Although the Security Council has a small membership compared with the General Assembly and tries to operate by consensus, it works most efficiently and effectively when one of the P5 exercises leadership. According to Jeffrey Laurenti, "The US is such a

Use of Force

From the UN Charter, Chapter VII

ARTICLE 42

Should the Security Council consider that measures provided for in Article 41 would be adequate or have proved to be inadequate, it may take such action by air, sea, or land forces as may be necessary to maintain or restore international peace and security. Such action may include demonstrations, blockades, and other operations by air, sea, or land forces of Members of the United Nations.

SECURITY COUNCIL COMPOSITION

Permanent Five (P5) members: China, France, Russia, United Kingdom, and United States
Nonpermanent members: three Africans, two Latin Americans, one Arab, one Asian, one Eastern European, and two Western Europeans

big power that it has enormous clout in the Security Council as its de facto 'majority, leader,' putting together the votes and resources to make things happen. The issues that arise there are generally those that most people and most governments acknowledge should be dealt with to some degree, and the United States is in a position to do things about them more than most members of the council." It follows from this clout that the United States can take a leading role in framing the council's agenda, especially when it sees advantages for its own international interests and policies. As Madeleine Albright notes, the UN's ability to intervene in certain emergencies often reduces the job of the United States: "This serves our interest because when the United States intervenes alone, we pay all of the costs and run all of the risks. When the UN acts, we pay a quarter of the costs and others provide the vast majority of troops."

The United Kingdom and France also play leading roles in the

Power Trip

"The Security Council is a body that is set up to reflect power and to use power to achieve ends in the real world. US power remains real even with our broken military and breaking economy because in the land of the blind, the one-eyed man remains at least a prince."
—Jeffrey Laurenti, Century Foundation

council. David Malone says they "work much harder than any of the other permanent members to come up with initiatives in areas far and wide. They send people of extraordinary skill to the council. . . . For these countries, their permanent membership really matters to their international identity precisely because their role in the world has shrunk. They're working very hard to stay permanent members of the Security Council."

The Russian Federation and China have emerged as important actors in the Security Council. Immediately after the breakup of the Soviet Union and the end of the Cold War, both nations tended to follow the US lead on the council, but in recent years they have staked out independent positions on certain key issues. "Russia sees its permanent seat as a very important piece of evidence that it's still a great power in the world," says former US ambassador John Bolton. Recently Russia has been a vocal council backer of its traditional friend, Serbia, which opposes any move by the UN to support independence for its Kosovo region. The other P5 members, knowing that the Russians have strong feelings on the matter and would veto any Security Council resolution deemed contrary to Serbian interests, have been reluctant to push the Kosovo issue. As Bolton notes, "That has had the consequence of driving the whole Kosovo issue right out of the Security Council." A similar dynamic appeared to be at work regarding the dispute between Russia and Georgia over a portion of Ossetia in the months following a conflict in August 2008 when no council action was taken.

China has also become more assertive in the council, says Bolton.

Fleeting Alliances

"There are many points of view in the Security Council, and there's no kind of permanent alliances between either side on anything. There are a series of key positions that need to be accommodated, and this is getting more scary for countries that don't have a clear sense of where they stand internationally or where their next aid check is coming from."
—Colin Keating, former New Zealand ambassador to the UN

"It's more active than I remember it was during the [George H. W.] Bush administration, when they had a largely passive role." Bolton sees China as more reserved than the other members of the P5, "but it's definitely changing and becoming more active, and there is every reason to think that tendency will continue." A highly visible instance of this occurred during the run-up to the Iraq War in 2003, when the Chinese refused to countenance any Security Council resolution that would condone the impending US invasion. The Chinese are especially sensitive to any UN resolutions that they believe interfere excessively in a nation's internal affairs. That was their justification for casting the veto with Russia, in 2008, against a US-sponsored resolution to impose sanctions on Zimbabwe's president and key personnel because of flawed national elections.

Larger countries are usually more active on the council than the smaller ones because they have the staff to keep up with the constantly increasing load. The number of annual meetings almost doubled between 1996 and 2007, from 114 to 202, while the number of resolutions adopted remained about the same (see table 1).

UN Sanctions

The Security Council is probably best known to the public for its role in creating peacekeeping missions to help stop international conflicts, but as will be noted in a later chapter, the members of the council prefer to start with less drastic means when they confront a conflict.

An Important Distinction

"You have to make a distinction between the UN as an institution and an organization, on the one hand, and the member states, particularly the Permanent Five, on the other. It's axiomatic that the solid achievements of the Security Council have tended to be when the P5 can act in harmony or consensus. If there is either strong disagreement or reluctance on the part of one or more of the P5 members, that's when you start getting into difficulties."
—John Negroponte, former US Ambassador to the UN

One of the Security Council's most frequently used tools to persuade a country or armed group to keep the peace is the sanction, a nonlethal, noninvasive mechanism aimed at preventing the party from interacting with the outside world in certain ways, such as engaging in trade or acquiring arms. Travel bans and financial or diplomatic restrictions are also types of sanction. According to Ban Ki-moon, experience has shown that sanctions work best as a means of persuasion, not punishment. "There is ample evidence that sanctions have enormous potential to contribute to the maintenance of international peace and security when used not as an end in themselves but in support of a holistic conflict resolution approach that includes prevention, mediation, peacekeeping, and peacebuilding. We should welcome the evolution of sanctions that has taken place: where once they were an often blunt and unfocused instrument, today they have become a more precise tool."

Sweeping Iraq Sanctions

Sanctions have a long history at the UN but did not become common until the 1990s, when they seemed to offer an efficient and inexpensive way of pressuring nations and groups that threaten international peace and security. Soon it became evident, however, that sanctions might unintentionally harm civilians, too. Sometimes the poorest or most vulnerable members of society were most harmed when their nation was placed under a sanction, especially one affecting trade and

Sanctions

From the UN Charter, Chapter VII

ARTICLE 41

The Security Council may decide what measures not involving the use of armed force are to be employed to give effect to its decisions, and it may call upon the Members of the United Nations to apply such measures. These may include complete or partial interruption of economic relations and of rail, sea, air, postal, telegraphic, radio, and other means of communication, and the severance of diplomatic relations.

commerce. Consider the case of Saddam Hussein's authoritarian regime in Iraq after the Gulf War.

When Iraq invaded Kuwait in 1990, the UN imposed sweeping sanctions intended to bar the aggressor from all foreign trade and financial dealings, except for humanitarian purposes. After the United States and its allies, with the UN's blessing, routed the Iraqi armed forces and arranged a cease-fire (which the UN monitored) in 1991, the UN left the sanctions in place while stipulating that Iraq divest itself of weapons of mass destruction. Because the Iraqi government was not fully cooperating with inspections, the UN continued the sanctions throughout the years of the Saddam Hussein regime.

The Iraqi government was able to evade some of the sanctions while complaining noisily and hypocritically that its citizens were being deprived of access to vital medicines, food, and other necessities. This effective campaign influenced the Security Council to create the Oil-for-Food Programme, which gave the Iraqi government the option of exporting specified amounts of crude oil, under UN scrutiny, to pay for "humanitarian goods." Terms of the program were liberalized in 1998 and 1999 and again in 2002 to give Iraq access to most civilian goods. The last liberalization was done through a Security Council resolution offered by the United States in May 2002. The idea behind the resolution was to enable Iraqi citizens to get necessities more easily while making it harder for Saddam Hussein's regime to use trade to obtain arms and other forbidden items. On May 22, 2003, two months after the US-led invasion of Iraq, the Security Council lifted sanctions except for the sale of weapons and related materiel.

Targeted Sanctions

The unsatisfactory dealings with the Saddam Hussein regime led the Security Council to refine its ideas about sanctions and give them more bite with less harm to innocent parties. One early beneficiary of the new approach was the African nation of Angola, where a guerrilla army called UNITA was disrupting a peace process arranged by the UN. In 1993 the council began hitting UNITA with a series of escalating sanctions, involving arms, petroleum, travel, and diamond sales and exports. At first, the world community did not adequately support the sanctions, and they had little effect, but things changed in 1999, when Canada assumed the chair of the Angolan sanctions committee. The Canadians prodded the committee to enforce the sanctions, and the prodding continued when Ireland succeeded Canada as chair. The pressure worked: the world community began to honor the sanctions, and UNITA found it increasingly difficult to obtain arms and other necessities. When its leader, Jonas Savimbi, was killed in 2002, the conflict finally ended.

To give the concept of targeted sanctions some specificity, consider the elements of Security Council Resolution 1718, passed only days after North Korea tested a nuclear device on October 9, 2006. The test violated terms of the Nuclear Test Ban Treaty, which the North Korean government had signed, and was done against the expressed wishes of the council. Members of the council were especially alarmed because North Korea had also been testing medium-range missiles capable of transporting nuclear warheads—which raised a nightmare scenario of nuclear proliferation, placing powerful weapons in the hands of an unpredictable rogue regime.

Resolution 1718 passed unanimously. It mandated that the Democratic People's Republic of Korea (North Korea) should "suspend all

US Ambassador John Bolton addresses the Security Council on North Korean sanctions, October 14, 2006. UN Photo/Eskinder Debebe

Countries Subject to UN Sanctions as of October 2008

Afghanistan
Côte d'Ivoire
Democratic People's Republic of Korea (North Korea)
Democratic Republic of the Congo
Iran
Iraq
Lebanon
Liberia
Sierra Leone
Somalia
Sudan

activity related to its ballistic missile program, abandon all nuclear weapons and programs, and abandon all weapons of mass destruction in a complete, verifiable, and irreversible manner." Representatives of various governments addressed the council after the vote, and almost all of them pointedly noted that the sanctions were not an end in themselves but a means to persuade North Korea to change its behavior, in which case the sanctions would be lifted. Speakers also emphasized that the sanctions were meant to put pressure on North Korea's leaders, not its citizens. As the British ambassador said, the resolution was "targeted at stopping the weapons of mass destruction and missile programmes and changing the behavior of those in authority in Pyongyang. It is not aimed at the people of North Korea, who are already suffering greatly."

The nature of the sanction's targeting becomes apparent when we look at the list of prohibited materials and actions (table 2). The list begins, predictably, with a section called "Arms Embargo," which requires UN member states to prevent the North Korean government from obtaining such military equipment as combat aircraft and warships, as well as technical training or services related to them.

Then, in the next section, luxury items are listed as a prohibited category, as if fancy chocolates and fine whiskey represented a threat to world peace. What was the Security Council thinking? After the sanctions vote and the ensuing speeches, many ambassadors and staffers were trading quips about how the ban on luxury goods would hit the Pyongyang government officials "where it hurt," in their collective sweet tooth. North Korea's leader, Kim Jong-il, and his cronies are notorious for coveting expensive imported delicacies and goods, exactly the kinds of products that ordinary Koreans cannot afford to buy even if they had access to them. So in that sense, the ban on luxury goods was as finely targeted as the ban on combat aircraft, and perhaps even more effective in changing official behavior!

After luxury goods, the sanctions list the freezing of certain financial assets and then move on to another targeted item, personal travel. Kim Jong-il really enjoys getting out of Pyongyang and taking trips to visit his neighbors in China, where he can stretch his legs and pose for the press. That became impossible with passage of the sanctions.

The Security Council meets to tighten sanctions on Iran, March 24, 2007.
UN Photo/Mark Garten

The council has also imposed similar sanctions on another would-be nuclear power, Iran, for failing to stop a uranium enrichment program despite passage of a Security Council resolution demanding its cessation. Like North Korea, Iran has tested medium-range missiles that could carry an atomic warhead, and it is possible that at some future date Iran will enter the club of nuclear powers, contrary to the provisions of the Nuclear Test Ban Treaty, which the Tehran government has signed. One of the strongest supporters of the Iran sanctions was the US government, which has consistently favored the well-targeted sanction as "an important tool to prompt change or behavior of regimes that threaten international peace and security," to quote a recent State Department report.

Although the imposition of sanctions does not involve the use of force, it is nevertheless a serious matter and can produce lengthy debate in the council. US ambassador John Danforth got a fast lesson about this in 2004, shortly after he assumed office, when he began urging the Security Council to stop the violence in Sudan's Darfur

Table 2. Summary List of Sanctions against North Korea, October 2006

Measure	Description
Arms embargo	1. Member states shall prevent the direct or indirect supply, sale, or transfer to the DPRK of: i. Any battle tanks, armored combat vehicles, large-caliber artillery systems, combat aircraft, attack helicopters, warships, missiles or missile systems, including technical training or services related to those items; ii. All items, materials, equipment, goods, and [nuclear] technology as set out in the lists in [three specified documents], including technical training or services related to those items. 2. DPRK shall cease the export of all items covered in paragraphs (i) and (ii) above, and all Member States shall prohibit the procurement of such items from the DPRK.
Luxury goods embargo	Member states shall prevent the direct or indirect supply, sale, or transfer to the DPRK of luxury goods.
Assets freeze	Member States shall freeze immediately the funds, other financial assets, and economic resources that are owned or controlled by individuals and entities designated by the Committee or by the Security Council as being engaged in or providing support for DPRK's nuclear-related, other weapon-of-mass-destruction-related, and ballistic-missile-related programs.
Travel ban	Member States shall take the necessary steps to prevent the entry into or transit through their territories of the persons designated by the Committee or by the Security Council as being responsible for DPRK policies in relation to the DPRK's nuclear-related, ballistic-missile-related, and other weapons-of-mass-destruction-related programs, together with their family members.

Source: http://www.un.org/sc/committees/1718/index.sthml

region. There, militias said to be acting with government backing had been attacking unarmed civilians. Danforth reasoned that the threat of international sanctions might push the government of Sudan to rein in the militias, so he raised the sanctions issue in the Security Council. Several of the Permanent Five resisted, however, and so Danforth had to switch tactics and press instead for "measures," under Article 41 of the Charter. "It's six of one and half a dozen of the other to say 'measures' instead of 'sanctions,'" he remarked philosophically. "The reality is that there are not going to be sanctions that are going to be applied against the government of Sudan. We're going to have sanctions but we can't use the word 'sanction.' To me it's a lesson in how the council works. It's difficult to get a strong resolution in the Security Council because of the nine-vote minimum and because all the permanent members have to sign on. But that's not to say you can't do some good, which we have."

Other Ways of Thinking about Security

Traditionally, the Security Council has viewed security as an issue of physical assault. The Universal Declaration of Human Rights, however, lists an array of securities, among them freedom from hunger, the right to adequate housing and decent employment, and the right to live in a healthy environment (see appendix B). Does the Security Council also oversee these forms of security? Historically the answer has been no. Rather, the council has left these matters to other parts of the UN system, especially the General Assembly, various agencies, programs, and commissions established to address issues like food supply, disaster relief, and health care.

This has its logic, because the Security Council imagines itself as an executive body more than an administrative system. However, the council did formally address a health-related issue on the grounds that vital security interests were at stake. US ambassador Richard Holbrooke set a precedent by persuading the Security Council to discuss the impact of the AIDS crisis in Africa in January 2000 at a meeting chaired by vice president Al Gore. A State Department report notes that although the discussion was "controversial at the time," it set the stage for a later council meeting and resolution about AIDS and caused language about HIV/AIDS to be included in peacekeeping resolutions.

The council entered another emerging area of threat in April 2007, when it debated climate change, specifically global warming. The day-long meeting was called by the United Kingdom to examine the relationship among energy needs, security, and climate. More than fifty delegations spoke, and although they generally agreed on the need for action about climate change, they disagreed on whether the Security Council was the right venue for discussing the issue. The representative from China made the point that even though climate change might have security implications, it was essentially an issue of sustainable economic development. He proposed that further discussions about the topic should be conducted in the appropriate international forums, using such established frameworks as the Kyoto Protocol. The Egyptian representative declared that the issue of climate change actually lay within the mandate of other UN bodies, specifically the General Assembly and the Economic and Social Council.

Several other representatives made a similar point, and in doing so they were alluding to a growing point of disagreement among member states. The expanded concept of security has been greeted as a welcome change by major powers, especially the United States, which see the council as the most effective place to address many of the world's most pressing problems. Among developing nations, however, the attitude is often very different. Pakistan's former permanent representative, Munir Akram, criticizes the council for encroaching on territory that he claims the Charter reserves to the General Assembly, which is dominated by the voting power of the less developed nations. During the past decade, he asserts, the Security Council has "begun to assume many functions that were originally intended for the General Assembly."

Council resolutions now address such issues as terrorism, nonproliferation, civilians in armed conflict, and violence against women and children. In October 2006, for example, the council debated the role of women in the consolidation of peace. The United States gave

Security Council members confer during a debate about energy, security, and climate issues, April 17, 2007. UN Photo/Evan Schneider

examples of how women have contributed to peace processes in places throughout the world, including Sierra Leone, the Democratic Republic of the Congo, and Nepal. The council also urged that peacekeeping operations take better account of gender issues and encouraged member states to place more women in peacekeeping operations.

The council's debate on gender related directly to peacemaking and peacekeeping, which are historic concerns of the UN. Munir Akram argues, however, that "these issues belong to the General Assembly. They are not part of the mandate of the Security Council, which is very tightly described in the Charter, which says the Security Council is the primary organ, not the sole organ, responsible for the *maintenance* of international peace and security and to respond to threats to international peace and security." Strictly speaking, says Akram, the council should not be addressing "sector issues," such as terrorism or proliferation, "where there is no imminent threat to peace." So, for example, he has no problem with Security Council Resolution 1267 against al-Qaeda and the Taliban, "but beyond that, to deal with the systemic issue of terrorism as a phenomenon, that is something that rightly should be addressed by the entire membership."

Ambassador Akram's critique does not receive much media coverage in the United States and other developed countries, but it is an important part of the growing "North-South" tension within the UN that fuels much of the dynamic between the council and the General Assembly. The preference of Akram and his colleagues to describe the dynamic as one between the wealthy nations, on one hand, and the less affluent or poor nations, on the other, gives the discussion a remarkably social and economic class flavor, but applied to the entire globe. We will return to it in the next chapter.

Reforming the Security Council

In recent years, many UN member states have begun urging a change of the Security Council to make it more reflective of today's international realities. Since the council was created in 1945, more than a hundred nations have come into existence, former pariah states like Japan, Germany, and South Africa have rejoined the world community, and many developing nations have become economic and trade dynamos.

Formal debates about reform have occurred in the General Assembly, and informal discussions occur everywhere in the UN system as participants advance their agendas and seek allies. "Reform" is a loaded word because its meaning is often so subjective and because any significant change will affect power relations and the status of particular member states. One suggested change is to expand the number of council members. The Japanese, who would like to gain a permanent seat, have suggested raising the number of members from fifteen to twenty-four and possibly restricting the veto.

Some insiders wonder if the reform advocates fully understand the impact of their proposed changes. "Any expansion risks making the council unworkable because it would become so big," claims Nancy Soderberg. "If you expand it you will just have more side groups to

Security Council ministerial-level meeting on the Middle East, September 21, 2006. UN/DPI Photo/M. Grant

work out things. You can't have an efficient body and negotiate with twenty-six people on it." Responding to Germany's well-known desire for a permanent seat, she cautions that the Europeans shouldn't have so many seats, especially now that they are part of the European Union: "How can you argue for four European countries on the council when Africa and Asia get one? . . . You're not going to have meaningful council expansion until you have a rotating EU seat with a veto." She argues that such changes won't happen soon, because the member states that must agree on it "are not going to put themselves out of power, nor will the United States work to get rid of its two best allies, France and the United Kingdom, in the council."

Secretary-General Ban Ki-moon has been urging the member states to tackle a restructuring of the council, something he describes as an "urgently needed reform." The United States has suggested that it could support an expanded council, including consideration of new permanent seats for Japan and a few developing countries. However, the United States wants no change in the status or privileges of the existing Permanent Five as outlined in the UN Charter, including any limitations on the veto.

Even if the United States were to embrace reform of the council enthusiastically, reform might not happen soon, owing to the sharp differences of opinion among member states about which of them should be admitted to an enlarged council. Members of major regional groupings, such as Africa or Asia, have been unable to agree on which of them should be selected for a permanent council seat. Former New Zealand ambassador Colin Keating speculates that India, South Africa, and Brazil seem ready to "hold out another ten years, if necessary, to get a whole cake. And in the meantime it's actually in their interest to see the UN become less effective as a kind of warning to everyone that 'We are big players and have to be accommodated.'" He adds quickly that these aspirant nations are not "working to undermine the legitimacy of the Security Council." On the other hand, "They are playing a leading role in ensuring that other aspects of UN reform aren't achievable in a major way, and thereby sending signals that the whole of the organization must be valued, and the whole of the membership's needs must be accommodated in some way, rather than trying to do little bits and pieces that are seen as important by a few countries."

One aspirant nation is Pakistan, whose former permanent representative, Munir Akram, analyzes the reform push as relying on several factors, beginning with the desire of "certain countries who think that they have now graduated to become great powers, to get a seat at the high table." Another factor is "the determination of those who have the power now, sitting at the high table, not to broaden the table too much except for their closest friends." The rest of the UN membership, consisting mainly of poor countries, "is worried that the oligarchy of power is going to be extended, at their expense, and that they will remain the proletariat while this extended oligarchy will continue to rule." These "proletarians" have no major national interest for rooting for one side or the other, although "the high-ranking powers are able to influence some small countries to support them."

Because the small countries have their power base in the General Assembly, that is usually where the influencing occurs. The assembly has a committee with the catchy name of the Open-Ended Working Group on the Question of Equitable Representation on and Increase in the Membership of the Security Council. UN insiders often refer to it as the *Never-Ending* Open-Ended Working Group on the Question of Equitable Representation on and Increase in the Membership of the Security Council, because it has met for more than a decade without reaching a consensus on a "framework resolution" for consideration by the full assembly. Brian Urquhart is not surprised at the lack of consensus. A UN insider since the organization's earliest days, Urquhart is convinced that Security Council reform is not easy and for a single, simple reason: "National prestige makes it extremely difficult to arrange." Maybe so, but the question of when and how the council might be changed seems to fascinate many Americans. Whenever I speak before groups of students and other members of the public, I am invariably asked for an opinion on this thorny issue, one that the Never-Ending Open-Ended Working Group is still pondering.

CHAPTER 6

The General Assembly and ECOSOC

Chapter IV, Article 9
1. The General Assembly shall consist of all the Members of the United Nations.

Chapter X, Article 62
1. The Economic and Social Council may make or initiate studies and reports with respect to international economic, social, cultural, educational, health, and related matters and may make recommendations with respect to any such matters to the General Assembly, to the Members of the United Nations, and to the specialized agencies concerned. —UN Charter

Today's media focus on the Security Council and secretary-general often obscures two other principal organs of the United Nations. Yet these two bodies were originally among the organization's most visible and active elements. When, for example, the UN wanted to give formal approval to the Universal Declaration of Human Rights in 1948, it sent the document to the General Assembly, the UN's main representative and deliberative body. And years before, when the UN had to arrange for the writing of the Declaration, the process was set

The General Assembly chamber. UN Photo/John Isaac

in motion by the Economic and Social Council, or ECOSOC. Gradually, however, the UN's center of gravity has been shifting elsewhere, to the Security Council and to some of the large agencies and commissions, such as the World Bank and the World Health Organization (discussed later). The shift, as noted in the previous chapter, has been part of a growing North-South rift within the UN.

More and Less than Meets the Eye

The General Assembly is both more and less than it appears. Although modeled on national parliaments, it has a global purview and visibility that no national legislature can match. It is a center for discussion and debate for the UN's 192 member states, with each having one vote.

Despite the assembly's global representation, its resolutions are binding only when they apply to internal UN matters. The UN Charter assigns the General Assembly responsibility for considering any

From the UN Charter, Chapter IV

1. The General Assembly may consider the general principles of co-operation in the maintenance of international peace and security, including the principles governing disarmament and the regulation of armaments, and may make recommendations with regard to such principles to the Members or to the Security Council or to both.
2. The General Assembly may discuss any questions relating to the maintenance of international peace and security brought before it by any Member of the United Nations, or by the Security Council, or by a state which is not a Member of the United Nations in accordance with Article 35, paragraph 2, and, except as provided in Article 12, may make recommendations with regard to any such questions to the state or states concerned or to the Security Council or to both. Any such question on which action is necessary shall be referred to the Security Council by the General Assembly either before or after discussion. . . .

ARTICLE 13

1. The General Assembly shall initiate studies and make recommendations for the purpose of:
a. promoting international co-operation in the political field and encouraging the progressive development of international law and its codification;
b. promoting international co-operation in the economic, social, cultural, educational, and health fields, and assisting in the realization of human rights and fundamental freedoms for all without distinction as to race, sex, language, or religion. . . .

ARTICLE 17

1. The General Assembly shall consider and approve the budget of the Organization.
2. The expenses of the Organization shall be borne by the Members as apportioned by the General Assembly.

3. The General Assembly shall consider and approve any financial and budgetary arrangements with specialized agencies referred to in Article 57 and shall examine the administrative budgets of such specialized agencies with a view to making recommendations to the agencies concerned.

issue that relates to a UN body or agency. The assembly commissions studies about international law, human rights, and all forms of international social, economic, cultural, and educational cooperation. It controls the purse strings, approves budgets, and decides how much each member state should contribute. It also elects the rotating members of the Security Council, as well as the members of ECOSOC and the Trusteeship Council. In collaboration with the Security Council, it elects the judges of the International Court of Justice and appoints the secretary-general.

Under some conditions the Security Council may ask the General Assembly to meet in special session, and such sessions can also be requested by a majority of member states. Issues deemed more pressing may warrant an emergency special session of the assembly, convened on twenty-four hours' notice at the request of the Security Council or a majority of member states.

General Assembly Ceremonies and Procedures

The General Assembly starts its official year with opening sessions, usually on the third Tuesday of each September. A week later, at the General Debate, which typically lasts about two weeks, heads of state address the assembly on important issues. It is an impressive sight to see the gathering of nearly two hundred heads of state and high dignitaries, many wearing national garb. (For a list of member states, see appendix C.) Then the members get down to substantive work, which lasts until mid-December. A two-tier system governs voting. Important matters like budgets and admission of new members require a two-thirds majority vote to pass, whereas others need only a simple

Pope Benedict XVI at the General Assembly, April 18, 2008. UN Photo/Mark Garten

majority. If, as often happens, the leadership can establish a consensus on a given matter, a formal vote may not even be needed.

General Assembly affairs are marked by a consuming passion for giving every member state some part of the action. There is a strong feeling that everyone should participate in as many decisions, committees, and issues as possible. As longtime UN insider Jeffrey Laurenti observes, "The UN is not a place where the notion of the small getting out of the way of the bigger has much traction. There is a high premium on schmoozing small and mid-level states." The parliamentary and administrative structure of the assembly reflects and embodies this need. At the beginning of each new General Assembly session, the members elect a president, twenty-one vice presidents (yes, twenty-one!), and the heads of the six Main Committees that largely run the assembly.

Regional and national rivalries feed the politically charged voting for these positions. To keep peace among members, formal and informal mechanisms ensure that the prerogatives and rewards of office are spread around. The presidency, for example, is rotated annually according to geographical region. If an Eastern European member state has the presidency one year, it must go to another region the next year. This produces a certain inefficiency that is tolerated because of its perceived greater good.

Committees of the General Assembly

The speeches and debates of the full General Assembly often make good media events and excellent political theater, but they are not necessarily effective means of examining issues in depth and arriving at solutions. For that, the assembly relies heavily on a clutch of committees: a General Committee, a Credentials Committee, and six Main Committees. Committees are common in legislatures worldwide because they enable many issues to be examined simultaneously. In the US Congress, committees consider legislation in the form of "bills," which become "laws" when passed by the House and Senate and signed by the president. General Assembly committees call their bills "resolutions." Each committee deliberates during the assembly session, votes on issues by simple majority, and sends its draft resolutions to the full assembly for a final vote. General Assembly resolutions, even when passed by vote, are basically recommendations, not laws, and are not binding.

The General Committee consists of the president, the twenty-one vice presidents, and the heads of the other committees. The Credentials Committee is responsible for determining the accredited General Assembly representatives of each member state. This is usually a pro

Six Main Committees of the General Assembly

First Committee, Disarmament and National Security
Second Committee, Economic and Financial
Third Committee, Social, Humanitarian, and Cultural
Fourth Committee, Special Political and Decolonization
Fifth Committee, Administrative and Budgetary
Sixth Committee, Legal

forma matter except when a nation is divided by civil war and two delegations claim the same seat. Then this normally unobtrusive committee becomes the locus of intense politicking and high emotion. An example involved Afghanistan, where the sitting delegation was challenged by the Taliban regime when it seized power. The Credentials Committee listened to presentations by both sides and then "deferred consideration," effectively confirming the old delegation without explicitly rejecting the claim of the other one. Such sidestepping, or action through inaction, is a classic political ploy.

Each of the six Main Committees has both a number and a name, and either may be used to describe it, but insiders usually use only the number. First Committee (Disarmament and International Security) considers resolutions about global security and weapons of mass destruction, as well as more conventional weapons. Second Committee (Economic and Financial) is responsible for examining economic and social development and international trade, including the reduction of barriers that prevent developing nations from reaching their full export potential. Third Committee (Social, Humanitarian, and Cultural) is concerned with a hodgepodge of issues ranging from disaster relief to human rights. It also deals with international crime, including drugs, human trafficking, and money laundering, as well as government and business corruption. Fourth Committee (Special Political and Decolonization), despite its name, no longer addresses decolonization because there are no more colonies. Instead, it has made peacekeeping its primary mission. The committee also has oversight of the

Symbolic Logic

"The General Assembly unfortunately has become a fairly useless body. At the symbolic level, it represents universality at the UN. All countries of the world virtually, even Switzerland now, are members of it. But the way it works has meant that it rarely takes meaningful decisions, and it takes so many un-meaningful decisions that it has been largely written off by the media.

"There's one significant function of the General Assembly. It serves as the umbrella for treaty negotiations on everything from the International Criminal Court to treaties on climate change, biodiversity, you name it. The treaties matter tremendously in the conduct of international relations."

—David Malone, former Canadian ambassador to the UN

United Nations Relief and Works Agency for Palestine Refugees in the Near East (UNRWA). Fifth Committee (Administrative and Budgetary) oversees the UN's fiscal affairs, and it drafts the resolutions for the general budget that the General Assembly votes on. Sixth Committee (Legal) oversees important legal issues, such as human cloning, international terrorism, and war crimes.

The World's Conference Host

The General Assembly also hosts conferences, many of which have played a key role in guiding the work of the UN since its inception (which occurred at a conference in San Francisco in 1945). Since 1994, the UN has held approximately one hundred conferences (through 2007) around the world on a variety of issues. Recent high-profile meetings on development issues have put long-term, difficult problems like poverty and environmental degradation atop the global agenda. In an effort to make the meetings into global forums that will shape the future of major issues, the UN has encouraged participation of thousands of nongovernmental organizations (NGOs), experts, and

World leaders at the 2005 summit. UN Photo/Eskinder Debebe

others not formally associated with the UN. A landmark conference that continues to redefine the UN's mission is the Millennium Summit in September 2000 and its accompanying Millennium Assembly (September 12–December 23, 2000). The lofty Millennium Development Goals, which all member states have agreed to meet by 2015, are discussed in chapter 15.

Criticism of the General Assembly

The assembly's culture favors moving through consensus, which takes time when nearly two hundred delegates are involved. Nancy Soderberg and other insiders accustomed to the relative speed and decisive-

ness of the Security Council chafe at the inefficient and polarized approach in the General Assembly, which they attribute to two large voting blocs, the Nonaligned Movement (NAM) and the Group of 77 (G-77). The Nonaligned Movement emerged during the Cold War, when the United States and the Soviet Union competed for influence in the world emerging through decolonization. Most NAM members were more closely associated with the Soviet Union than the United States, recalls Pakistan's former permanent representative, Munir Akram, but now "the NAM is more nonaligned than formerly." One member, India, regards itself as a major world power, whereas China, which certainly sees itself as a major power, is not a member of the Nonaligned Movement but works closely with it.

The Group of 77, says Akram, "was created for very limited purposes, at the time of the first conference at the UN held to coordinate
the position of developing countries on trade and development issues," during the era of decolonization. The group gradually acquired
a sense of identity. "There is diversity in this group," Akram says, "but
there is a sense that on systemic issues of international economic
relations their interests are not identical, but convergent, in the sense
that all of them have an interest to change the present system of trade,
finance, and technology control, because they feel that it is weighted
against them or structured in ways that place them at a disadvantage."
Equally important, the G-77 has grown in membership to 130, enough
to control voting in the General Assembly.

The presence of these two blocs governs the pace and nature of
assembly deliberations and decisions. Nancy Soderberg complains
that "it's very difficult to be in the General Assembly because everything is done by consensus, so it's the lowest common denominator
of 192 different countries, which is a pretty low standard." This means
that the assembly effectively cedes decisive action to the Security
Council. As Soderberg says, "Everyone pretends that they don't want
to be run by the Security Council, but the key agenda is run by the
council. The assembly can put out resolutions on laudatory, amor-
phous goals, but if you're really going to have an impact and do things,
do it through the Security Council."

Soderberg accuses the blocs of being out of step with current realities. "Look at the Nonaligned Movement," she says. "What are they
nonaligned against now? There is no alignment, which means that
they are really trying to oppose the United States more often than not,
which makes no sense." Richard Holbrooke shares her exasperation.
The Nonaligned Movement and the G-77 do tremendous damage
because they "just don't serve the interests of most of their members.
They are two groups that are pulled by old-school politics."

A very different view comes from Pakistan's Ambassador Akram,
who recently held a term as head of the G-77. He begins by noting that
the General Assembly is being marginalized by the Security Council's
continual accumulation of power. While admitting some of the criticisms leveled at the assembly—"their resolutions are too long, there

The Trusteeship Council

Of the six principal organs of the UN, the Trusteeship Council is the least well known, and for good reason. On November 1, 1994, it suspended operations and ceased to exist except on paper. The demise of the council is part of the UN's important role in decolonization, the process by which some eighty nations have come into existence since 1945. When decolonization began, most of Africa was controlled by a few Western nations, while the Netherlands, United Kingdom, and France ruled large parts of Asia. Japan had ruled Korea for half a century. Scattered around the world, alongside the colonies, were territories, such as Papua, New Guinea, and the Mariana Islands in the Pacific, that had been wards of the League of Nations and were now administered by Australia, the United States, and other nations. Article 75 of the Charter states that "the United Nations shall establish under its authority an international trusteeship system for the administration and supervision of such territories as may be placed there under by subsequent individual agreements. These territories are hereinafter referred to as trust territories." The UN wanted to ensure that trustee nations would truly look after the best interests of their charges and help them secure self-government, either on their own or as parts of larger entities. Palau, an island group in the Pacific, was the last trust territory. It became a UN member on December 15, 1994.

are too many reports, there are too many items—that's all true"—he responds that "the same could be said of the Security Council," which "repeats many things that are in previous resolutions." Akram further argues that the Nonaligned Movement and the Group of 77 are potentially vehicles for positive change. The G-77 "can often coordinate its position and take common positions," and it benefits also from a new sense of confidence among the developing countries, in part because a number of them have had successful economic growth and a number are so-called emerging economies. From Akram's perspective, the NAM and the G-77 can potentially contribute to the UN's evolution, as well as to global social and economic development.

Just as clearly, former US permanent representative John Bolton says the regional bloc system "is a contributing factor to the ineffectiveness of the UN because it helps reinforce the status quo and becomes a way for countries to protect and get part of the benefits that accrue from the UN programs. It leads to a scratch-my-back-and-I'll-scratch-yours philosophy. That makes it unlikely you're gong to have very effective change or reform."

Ironically, most of the nations that constitute the G-77 came into existence because of a global movement that the United States strongly supported. The word "decolonization" was on everyone's lips from the 1950s through the 1970s, when some eighty new nations emerged as several great powers, notably the United Kingdom, France, and Japan, lost their empires. After World War II, nationalist uprisings and resistance movements quickly challenged the colonial world order and forced out the ruling nations or persuaded them to relinquish authority.

The United States encouraged the UN to be a key player in ending colonization. In fact, one of the most important UN staff members working on anticolonialism was an African American diplomat, Ralph Bunche, who had joined the State Department in 1945 and worked in the San Francisco conference that helped organize the UN that spring.

Insider Brian Urquhart, who knew Bunche well, describes him as the "dynamo" of the decolonization movement "because he knew more about it than anybody else did, including most European colonial experts." Secretary-General Trygve Lie assigned him to the Middle East, where the UN was brokering Britain's withdrawal from its League of Nations mandate in Palestine while the resident Jewish population was laying foundations for the new state of Israel. For his central role in negotiating a general settlement among the Israelis, British, Egyptians, and other interested powers, Ralph Bunche was awarded the Nobel Peace Prize in 1950.

The end of colonialism changed the world, and much faster than anyone expected. Decolonization also transformed the UN. The original UN had fifty-one member states and operated like a small club. During the decades after 1945, the addition of so many new nations produced two powerful voting blocs, the Nonaligned Movement and the Group of 77, as noted above.

UN Days and Weeks of the Year

The UN year is marked by nearly sixty days and weeks that call attention to important world issues and provide the occasion for educational and public events both inside and outside the United Nations.

January 27—International Day of Commemoration in Memory of the Victims of the Holocaust

February 21—International Mother Language Day

March 8—United Nations Day for Women's Rights and International Peace

March 21—International Day for the Elimination of Racial Discrimination

March 21—Beginning Week of Solidarity with the Peoples Struggling Against Racism and Racial Discrimination

March 22—World Day for Water

March 23—World Meteorological Day

March 26—International Day for the Commemoration of the Two-Hundredth Anniversary of the Abolition of the Trans-Atlantic Slave Trade

April 4—International Day for Mine Awareness and Assistance in Mine Action

April 7—World Health Day

April 23—World Book and Copyright Day

April 23–29, 2007—United Nations Global Road Safety Week

May 3—World Press Freedom Day

May 8 and 9 —Time of Remembrance and Reconciliation for Those Who Lost Their Lives during the Second World War

May 15—International Day of Families

May 17—World Telecommunication Day

May 17—World Information Society Day

May 21—World Day for Cultural Diversity for Dialogue and Development

May 22—International Day for Biological Diversity

May 25—Beginning Week of Solidarity with the Peoples of Non-Self-Governing Territories

May 29—International Day of United Nations Peacekeepers

May 31—World No-Tobacco Day

June 4—International Day of Innocent Children Victims of Aggression

June 5—World Environment Day

June 17—World Day to Combat Desertification and Drought

June 20—World Refugee Day

June 23—United Nations Public Service Day

June 26—International Day Against Drug Abuse and Illicit Trafficking

June 26—International Day in Support of Victims of Torture

July—International Day of Cooperatives (first Saturday of July)

July 11—World Population Day

August 9—International Day of the World's Indigenous People

August 12—International Youth Day

August 23—International Day for the Remembrance of the Slave Trade and Its Abolition

September 8—International Literacy Day

September 16—International Day for the Preservation of the Ozone Layer

September 21—International Day of Peace

September—World Maritime Day (during last week of September)

October 1—International Day of Older Persons

October 4–10—World Space Week

October 5—World Teachers' Day

October—World Habitat Day (first Monday of October)

October—International Day for Natural Disaster Reduction (second Wednesday of October)

October 9—World Post Day

October 10—World Mental Health Day

October 16—World Food Day

October 17—International Day for the Eradication of Poverty

October 24—United Nations Day

October 24—World Development Information Day

October 24–30—Disarmament Week

November 6—International Day for Preventing the Exploitation of the Environment in War and Armed Conflict

November 14—World Diabetes Day

November 16—International Day for Tolerance

November—World Day of Remembrance for Road Traffic Victims (third Sunday of November)

November 20—Africa Industrialization Day

November 20—Universal Children's Day

November 21—World Television Day

November 25—International Day for the Elimination of Violence Against Women

November 29—International Day of Solidarity with the Palestinian People

December 1—World AIDS Day

December 1—HIV Counseling and Testing Day (voluntary observation)

December 2—International Day for the Abolition of Slavery

December 3—International Day of Disabled Persons

December 5—International Volunteer Day for Economic and Social Development

December 7—International Civil Aviation Day

December 10—Human Rights Day

December 11—International Mountain Day

December 18—International Migrants Day

December 19—United Nations Day for South-South Cooperation

December 20—International Human Solidarity Day

The Economic and Social Council

The Economic and Social Council was intended to be a coordinator and mediator among the constituent bodies of the UN system. But it has struggled to define a clear identity among its many functions and has thus been accused of a lack of focus. Many insiders have remarked on ECOSOC's talent for fostering debate that leads to no apparent action. Admittedly, ECOSOC was created as a deliberative rather than an operational body, to help other parts of the UN system examine and shape their programs.

Counting the Hours

"The worst two years of my life were spent as Canada's representative of ECOSOC. A complete waste of time."
—David Malone, former Canadian ambassador to the UN

Its mandate is to function as a forum for discussing international social, economic, and humanitarian issues, as well as to coordinate the work of UN agencies and bodies concerned with those issues. As part of its coordinating role, ECOSOC commissions studies, writes reports, and makes policy recommendations to the General Assembly and other parts of the UN. Membership in ECOSOC—which holds a major session every July—is coveted, owing to the body's central role in the UN universe. Its fifty-four members, elected by the General Assembly, serve three-year terms.

Perhaps because its mission is so extensive and it does a lot of coordinating among groups and organizations, ECOSOC has suffered from a lack of conceptual and administrative focus. Many diplomats, like David Malone, have found the organization's fuzziness and endless discussions hard to endure. This has spawned recommendations for reworking the body.

Munir Akram believes that ECOSOC would be very functional and relevant if it had the same kind of binding authority on economic decisions that the Security Council has for political and security issues. "You have to empower ECOSOC," he asserts. "You have to see how to make it work in a system that is relevant to the real world." One can imagine Malone nodding in agreement but asking, How?

In 2005 Pakistan and several other countries proposed a way to update ECOSOC through two mechanisms. One is called the Annual Ministry of Review (AMR), and the other is the Development Cooperation Forum. The AMR would enable ECOSOC to hold annual meetings for reviewing international policies about trade and development, including the Millennium Development Goals. The AMR "should

The ECOSOC chamber. UN Photo/Andrea Brizzi

serve as a standing annual review body," says Akram. The Development Cooperation Forum, in contrast, is supposed to review the status of development cooperation within the UN system. These two new mechanisms are actually in process and will soon be rolled out to public viewing. If they succeed, Akram believes that "we will see a new policy approach to development cooperation across the whole UN system."

ECOSOC and Nongovernmental Organizations

An irony of ECOSOC's difficult evolution is that one of its most important and delicate tasks today was barely on the radar screen back in 1945 when the organization was created. ECOSOC is the intermediary between the General Assembly and nongovernmental organizations.

A Public-Private Partnership

"NGOs play a more and more important role not only in the policy debates but equally important, maybe even more important, are critical in implementing many of these policies. A lot of the aid and emergency humanitarian assistance, like food distribution by the World Food Program, is done through the NGOs. There really is a public-private partnership, or a public-NGO partnership, that is very important. NGOs are effective, and part of the reason is they are private and they are accountable; they watch their pennies. People have a choice as to whom to give their money."

—John Negroponte, former US ambassador to the UN

NGOs are independent, nonprofit groups that focus on one or more areas of interest to the UN. In the United States, we usually refer to them as "nonprofit organizations" because we make a sharp distinction between private enterprise (which is profit making) and civil society (which is not), but in most of the world, where the crucial distinction is between governmental and nongovernmental, NGO makes more sense as a category. (Outside the United States, business is often included in civil society, again because the crucial distinction is between governmental versus nongovernmental.)

When the UN was founded there were few NGOs, but their number worldwide has multiplied many times over since then. The UN has taken a growing interest in NGOs because they represent the interests of civil society, which is gaining visibility as a foundation of democracy. Kofi Annan acknowledged the importance of creating partnerships between the UN and civil society to achieve "a new synthesis between private initiative and the public good, which encourages entrepreneurship and market approaches together with social and environmental responsibility."

ECOSOC negotiates the agreements that define relations between the UN and the more than three thousand NGOs that have "consultative status," which gives them the right to participate in certain UN

From the UN Charter, Chapter X

1. The Economic and Social Council may make or initiate studies and reports with respect to international economic, social, cultural, educational, health, and related matters and may make recommendations with respect to any such matters to the General Assembly, to the Members of the United Nations, and to the specialized agencies concerned.
2. It may make recommendations for the purpose of promoting respect for, and observance of, human rights and fundamental freedoms for all.
3. It may prepare draft conventions for submission to the General Assembly, with respect to matters falling within its competence.
4. It may call, in accordance with the rules prescribed by the United Nations, international conferences on matters falling within its competence.

1. The Economic and Social Council may enter into agreements with any of the agencies referred to in Article 57, defining the terms on which the agency concerned shall be brought into relationship with the United Nations. Such agreements shall be subject to approval by the General Assembly.
2. It may coordinate the activities of the specialized agencies through consultation with and recommendations to such agencies and through recommendations to the General Assembly and to the Members of the United Nations.

New Thinking

"We cannot afford to be burdened with labels such as 'rich' or 'poor,' 'developed' or 'developing,' 'North' or 'South,' or 'the Non Aligned Movement.' In the twenty-first century these false divisions rarely serve anyone's interests. In facing challenges of the scale that lie before us, all peoples and nations should focus on what we have in common: our shared desire to live freely and securely, in health, with hope and with opportunity. Those are the interests and aspirations of the American people and they are shared by billions around the world."   —Susan E. Rice, US ambassador to the UN

meetings, studies, and projects and to submit reports to ECOSOC. Nongovernmental organizations may also serve as technical experts, advisers, and consultants to governments and the Secretariat. As advocacy groups they may support UN plans of action, programs, and declarations. Organizations qualifying for General Category consultative status may propose new items for ECOSOC's consideration.

Nongovernmental organizations have their own liaison body, the Conference on Non-Governmental Organizations in Consultative Status (CONGO), to represent their interests before ECOSOC and hold meetings about issues of common interest. Those NGOs holding consultative status remain independent bodies and do not become actual parts of the UN. To the contrary, their influence often depends on their reputation for independence from outside authority.

Nongovernmental organizations have become important in helping implement many UN efforts and programs such as those related to human rights, literacy, health care, and economic development. Insiders generally acknowledge that NGOs have greatly expanded the UN's reach and technical competence and serve a vital watchdog function.

CHAPTER 7

Rubbing Elbows and Egos in the UN Village

The amount of psychology in diplomacy is remarkable. States behave very much as human beings. It is very ego driven, I would say. We want to be there, we want to be where decisions are taken.

—Danilo Türk, former Slovenian ambassador to the UN and assistant secretary-general for political affairs

The United Nations is known for operating in ways that may seem complicated and convoluted. The Secretariat's administrators can have their intricate procedures and protocols, and they follow their proper, not always straight and narrow, channels. The same is true in the General Assembly, where red tape decorates resolutions, studies, reports, and memoranda. In the many UN-related bodies, agencies, and commissions, a passion for creating and filing paper does occasionally obscure the central point of the organization.

But just as often the UN is as simple and straightforward a place as can be imagined, because, as David Malone notes, "people really matter at the UN." Many experts who look at the UN's structure, procedures, and resolutions don't realize that "anything that happens at the UN happens because of certain individuals."

Malone calculates that "at any given time, out of 192 ambassadors, about thirty-five control the game. Within the Security Council four or five ambassadors at any given time are dominant, perhaps a few more, counting the nonpermanent ones. This is also true in each of the General Assembly committees." So, if you know those thirty-five key people, you can do anything. And if you don't, forget it.

When trying to understand the UN, it's also important not to confuse administrative problems with issues of governance and decision-making. When talk turns into decision and action, the procedures can be very different from what bureaucrats are accustomed to, and often that difference is the reason things get done. Governance and decision-making frequently involve levels of persuasion, guile, and gall that we would expect to find in a novel or movie about Wall Street.

The Village

Think of a small town where decisions are made by groups of key people who know one another and often socialize while standing at street corners or sipping coffee at a café. In fact, this is exactly how Richard Holbrooke describes his experience as US permanent representative under President Clinton. Looking back on those sixteen months in New York, he remembers a place he calls the UN Village. The village works through small groups, formal or informal, endless meetings, caucuses, speeches, and meals. "Food is probably the thing that holds the UN together," notes Holbrooke. "Boy, do those guys like to eat!"

Former US permanent representative John Negroponte also operated in the UN Village. "I've called on 114 delegates," he remarked when asked about his first few months at the UN. "I'm going to call on everyone that I'm allowed to call on. The diplomatic practice is that if you arrived after another delegate, then you go and call on them. If they've arrived after you have, then they go and see you. The new kid on the block comes around to see you."

Negroponte tried even harder to meet with regional groups, "because the regional groups are where a lot of the business of the UN is

Where to Find It

Located on the Upper East Side, the UN village has "its own language and time zone, where 'demand' means 'ask,' 'strong' means 'not so strong,' and 'severe' means 'not so severe,' and 'urges' means 'begs.' All a different lingo. Thousands of people live here who have very little interaction with the rest of the city."
—Richard Holbrooke, former US ambassador to the UN

done." He visited with the European Union "once every six or eight weeks" and with the South African Development Group, the Economic Council of West African States, and others. "Meeting with" can often mean drinks or dinner, sometimes at the elegant Waldorf-Astoria.

Within the UN Village are "neighborhoods," some of them pretty exclusive. Negroponte lived in one of the toniest, the Security Council. As he stated during his tenure, "Most of my dealings are in the Security Council, which is a fairly small and tight-knit group, and we meet each other one way or another every day. We get to know each other pretty well. And so there is a certain camaraderie in the Security Council." He also had to spend some time in that other part of town, the General Assembly, where crowds of ordinary nations mill about, shouting and waving their hands. "I think where the nerves sometimes get a little frayed around the edges is in some of these big

Diplomatically Speaking

"We're diplomats, so whatever feelings people may have they're going to be muted, guarded, and careful. I think most diplomats feel that you can disagree without being disagreeable. I think that's part of our work ethic, because otherwise you could live in quite unbearable circumstances."
—John Negroponte, former US ambassador to the UN

Representatives of China, Russia, and United States confer before a meeting
on Kosovo, February 18, 2008. UN Photo/Eskinder Debebe

General Assembly special sessions, particularly when you have to
reach consensus on a document. Nerves can get frayed and you have
these marathon meetings that go on until eight in the morning, and
you have NGOs in the bleachers that are pushing single-minded positions. But even there, particularly if you can succeed in achieving
consensus, if you can reach consensus on a document, I think there's
always a huge sense of relief even among those who were opposed to
positions we had. They can say to themselves, at least we produced
something at the end of this."

Like all villages, this one has its cliques and factions. For one thing,
the population is very male, a sort of diplomatic stag party of political
incorrectness. (By contrast, women do very well in many other parts of
the UN: in 2000, women represented over 53 percent of Americans in
professional and senior positions in the Secretariat and 44 percent of
Americans in all UN agencies.)

The few women who crash the party have described the experience
in various ways. Madeleine Albright, who was US permanent representative, remembers the thrill of being not just a woman in that

A Diplomat Rates the Media

"The professionalism among the reporters at the UN is one of my big discoveries at the Security Council. They knew the background, knew what to quote, and they also knew how to formulate an opinion. It was always very clear what is quotation, what is opinion, so I could rely on the reports from the local press. Sometimes things got tricky, on Iraq, on Kosovo. We had questions: What do you mean? Did you say that? And sometimes the one who comes to you with an accusation or interpretation can be trumped by the original report. So I took the reports from the newspaper or the press agency and said, 'Look that is what was reported, that is absolutely correct. It is your understanding or your explanation which creates a problem.' My respect for reporters grew exponentially as a result of such experiences. People who work here are very knowledgeable and are good reporters, so it's something that has to be respected."
—Danilo Türk, former Slovenian ambassador to the UN

environment but "the woman who represents the United States," the dominant power.

Other women representatives may not feel the power rush yet recall the special quality of life at a men's club. Nancy Soderberg remembers old-fashioned gallantry. "Being a woman there is interesting, particularly if you are on the Security Council, because there are no women on the Security Council." She enjoyed the men's attention. "One of the things that I just loved, being a young woman on the council, is that chivalry really does live there. They are so gentlemanly and just wonderful. At times they come up and kiss your hand and everyone stands up for you." Try that in the US Senate!

Security Council Politics

The UN Village is especially visible at the Security Council. Most member states regard participation on the council as advantageous, but not everyone sees it that way.

John Negroponte recalls that it took a while for Mexico to seek a council seat because were concerns that it would be a no-win situation. Some of his Mexican colleagues were thinking, "If we agree with the United States, then that will be taken for granted, and if we disagree with the United States, that will hurt us in our bilateral relationship with the United States." The Mexican president and others took the opposite tack, however, maintaining that Mexico needed to be more visible on the world stage and not worry about how the audience would react. Negroponte's Mexican counterparts asked him, "Will you hold it against Mexico if we take positions against the United States or at odds with the United States?" Negroponte replied with diplomatic aplomb, "Everything we do is going to be in the context of an excellent bilateral relationship. . . . We may have our differences, but it's a crucial relationship to us, and it's going to remain that, and we're going to deal with Mexico accordingly."

Mexico is not the only nation to hesitate before deciding to run for election to the Security Council. When the newly minted nation of Slovenia, once part of Yugoslavia, took stock of its diplomatic situation, one of the first matters considered was a possible candidacy for the Security Council. Danilo Türk was Slovenia's ambassador to the UN during the 1990s and Security Council president in August 1998. Later he was elected president of Slovenia. "I thought Slovenia would make a good show in the Security Council," he says, but that was not the universal opinion either in the UN or in Slovenia. "There was a debate whether or not we need that. Membership in the Security Council brings exposure to have to deal with issues that are very politically contested. It was not an easy decision, and I presented pluses and minuses." One of the pluses was that membership would strengthen the new nation's profile in the world community.

Finally Slovenia decided to throw its hat in the ring for the elections scheduled in 1997. But first the government had to decide which voting bloc it would run in. As always in the UN, a quota system ensures that each world region will have representation. In any given year, a certain number of places will open up for the Western Europe and Others Group or for the Latin American and Caribbean Group, for example, and countries in those regions will compete with one another for a seat. Sometimes the countries of a region will agree who should be elected to the open slots. At other times the countries will engage in a genuine political campaign involving arm-twisting, alliances, and occasional backstabbing.

The politics can get especially nasty if one nation finds the candidacy of another obnoxious. For example, in fall 2000, three Western European countries were fighting for two slots. According to news reports, Norway and Italy were "wining and dining decision-makers in New York and elsewhere," whereas the third candidate, Ireland, was appealing to developing countries in the General Assembly, "stressing its poor, former-colonial roots as proof that it understands their needs." The United States was not taking sides but was instead backing an African nation, Mauritius, in order to prevent Sudan, which was under Security Council sanctions, from becoming a Security Council member. The United States accused Sudan of massive human rights abuses and of having links with terrorists. African diplomats, however, were said to resent the Americans' strong-arm tactics, while others were claiming that the United States could have persuaded Sudan to withdraw its candidacy by offering to lift U.S. sanctions against Sudan. But the United States persisted and was rewarded when the General Assembly elected Mauritius, in the fourth round of voting, as one of five new Security Council members to serve in 2001 and 2002.

Danilo Türk did not face quite such high-powered politics when he guided Slovenia through its Security Council candidacy, but he did have to decide whether to campaign for the slot of Western Europe and Others or Eastern Europe. "Initially we didn't want to be a member of the Eastern European Group. We said we are geographically west of Vienna, we didn't think automatically that there should be any linkage between the former Yugoslavia membership in the Eastern European Group and Slovenian membership in the same group." The Slovenians later changed their minds "because we thought, it is important to get elected." They decided in 1996 to join the Eastern European Group, "where it is easier to get elected than the Western

US Ambassador John Bolton confers with the Guatemala delegation in the General Assembly, October 16, 2006. UN Photo/Marco Castro

because the competition is not as tough." Valuable time had passed, however, and there were two other candidates for the seat, Belarus and Macedonia. "Usually member states announce their candidature five years in advance, in some cases, ten or fifteen years in advance, and they campaign gradually. The last two years they campaign very intensely. Of course, if the seat is not contested, there is no campaign, but even then they have to talk to other members because they have to get two-thirds of the entire membership. We came very late and there were two other candidates, but I had to do it. Because if I didn't, I would be asked, 'Where were you, what were you doing?' Belarus withdrew at last minute, a couple of days before elections, because they had no chance. We defeated the remaining candidate. So that's how Slovenia became a member of the Security Council."

And it was worth it, says Türk, if only for the international publicity. "We discovered that half of what was important internationally about Slovenia related to the Security Council in those two years [1998–99]. For a small country, this is an incredible exposure."

> **Between Acts**
>
> "You see another side of these guys when you get them out of the formal setting. Wang is very interesting. He's very quiet, but if you get him alone, he's very curious and down to earth and more open than other Chinese reps I've seen. You can actually have an argument with him about Tibet."
> —Nancy Soderberg, former US ambassador to the UN

Türk makes a bigger, more interesting argument when he observes that smaller nations may not be as bound by rigid policies and positions as larger ones, giving them the opportunity to orchestrate some creative diplomacy where otherwise there might be conflict or confrontation. "If a country like Slovenia fails, it is no problem, but if a big country fails with a proposal, that usually has political repercussions. So small countries, nonpermanent members, can be constructive and genuinely helpful members of the Security Council. They can afford some imagination and experimentation. I always believed that. I never thought that only permanent members count." Jeffrey Laurenti largely agrees. "Smaller country reps are freer agents and operate like parliamentarians in the European parliament," he says.

Formally Informal or Informally Formal?

Once a member state becomes a player in a clique or faction, it needs to know the rules and procedures. One basic principle is that the most important business is done ostensibly in the open but actually in private. There's a reason why so many decisions, not just at the UN but in organizations the world over, are made by a few people in a back room. Chances are that if the terms of the agreement were discussed in public, with all the constraints of touchy issues, no one would agree to anything significant. So a common arrangement at the UN is to begin a debate or discussion in a large public setting, such as the Security Council chamber, and then, as the individual points become defined, to break up into smaller, less public groups. Finally, a few

Delegates confer in a second-floor lounge near the
General Assembly hall. UN Photo / Andrea Brizzi

people sitting at a table resolve the most contentious points, with no
media presence and sometimes with no one taking notes.

In the Security Council, the opening discussions are referred to as
the formals and the subsequent, less public talks as the informals.
Nancy Soderberg came to regard the formal meetings as "just a staged
show, there is just nothing that happens in them." Rather, the serious
negotiations happen at the informals, "because you can't negotiate in
a formal setting, you can't talk to people." Occasionally the formal
setting is good for sending signals to another member, but nothing
happens there. "For the most part, you go in, there's a briefing that
nobody pays attention to, and everyone reads prepared statements and
nothing happens."

> ## Reciprocity and Good Manners
>
> "One of the glories of the UN is that it is a system of multilateralism, which makes the reps of countries deal intimately with each other. This is retail global politics up close on the East River, so, as in a parliamentary system, niceness and conviviality count for a lot."
> —Mark Malloch Brown, former deputy secretary-general of the UN

Sometimes, though, even the informals are too formal for serious talk. "The informals are not so informal," says Soderberg. "It still is pretty formal because you have a chair who does everyone in order. It's really hard to have negotiations when you have to wait your turn." The actual decision may already have been made anyway. But where? "In the back room," says Soderberg.

Quids for Quos

There are few secrets in the UN Village. Everyone knows everyone else—not just their strengths and weaknesses but their quirks, too, as well as the sensitive places you don't touch unless you're prepared for a strong reaction. Surprises are still possible, though, especially when one member state, or group of states, steps across one of the invisible annoyance lines that surround every member like the isobars on a weather map.

China, for example, is known to be very ticklish on the question of Taiwan. But some Central American countries have long championed UN membership for Taiwan. Every year they introduce a resolution in the General Assembly to admit Taiwan, and every year it is defeated. "But it never fails to irritate the hell out of China," remarks David Malone. A few years ago, when Guatemala was ending its civil war and needed a UN peacekeeping operation, the Chinese vetoed it "as a signal to Guatemala that they simply wouldn't stand for Guatemala continuing to participate in this effort to legitimize Taiwan at the UN." So the Guatemalans met privately with the Chinese, "negotiated a reformulation of the Guatemala position on Taiwan that satisfied the Chinese, and the Chinese veto was lifted about ten days later."

Malone recalls another awkward moment involving Taiwan that occurred when the UN was engaged in a "preventive" deployment in Macedonia. "After a change of government in Macedonia—this was in 1998—a new government cozied up to Taiwan and was alleged to have accepted significant financial aid from Taiwan. When the mandate renewal of the UN preventive deployment came up, China vetoed it. It was denounced by other members of the Security Council for doing so, but naturally the Macedonian government should have known this would be the outcome of its cozying up to Taiwan."

CHAPTER 8

Keeping Tabs on How Nations Vote

A country's voting record in the United Nations is only one dimension of its relations with the United States. . . . Nevertheless, a country's behavior at the United Nations is always relevant in its bilateral relationship with the United States, a point the Secretary of State regularly makes in letters of instruction to new U.S. ambassadors. —US Department of State

We are hardly surprised to learn that because the United States is the biggest player at the United Nations, its words, actions, and non-actions are parsed in a hundred different ways by the world's media, governments, and analysts. But people are not generally aware that the US government does its own parsing of member states' behavior, especially their voting records. Because the US government places great importance on positioning itself strongly within the UN system, it monitors how other nations vote in the 192-member General Assembly and the fifteen-member Security Council. Section 406 of Public Law 101-246 requires the State Department to inform Congress annually about how UN member states have voted in comparison with the United States. Of course, the US ambassador and other staff have access to this information and can shape their words and actions accordingly.

Voting in the Security Council. UN Photo / Evan Schneider

Each year, the State Department's UN analysts tote up the issues and votes and then examine them according to several criteria, such as the geographical distribution of the member states (Europe, Asia, and so on) or their tendency to vote with or contrary to the US voting position. For the Security Council, there is usually no suspense about the numbers. The tight club almost always acts through consensus. In 2006–7, for example, the council considered fifty-seven resolutions and adopted fifty-six, many of them unanimously. The only vetoes during that span were cast by China and Russia on a resolution about Myanmar (Burma). John Negroponte sees the strong consensus numbers as clear proof that "for all the talk about how people worry and our being unilateral, the number of resolutions and issues that we succeed in dealing with on a totally consensus basis is really quite striking."

In the General Assembly the picture is very different. The Sixty-Second General Assembly (2006–7) adopted 246 resolutions, 170 (69 percent) by consensus. That means that in more than two-thirds

Tallying the vote in the General Assembly. UN Photo/Eskinder Debebe

of the votes, the United States and the rest of the assembly, representing the interests of 191 other nations, all voted the same way. That's remarkable, given the wide spectrum of perspectives, agendas, and interests in the assembly.

The interesting numbers concern the other one-third of the votes, the nonconsensus issues in which a vote was recorded. Here we can see how US interests often differ from those of other governments or blocs such as the Asian or African groups and the Group of 77, and to that extent we can see how the United States sits within the broader world community.

In the nonconsensus votes, the overall rate of coincidence varies greatly by issue, and even for the same issue the consensus may shift from year to year (see table 3). In 1999, for example, the United States and other UN members agreed more than half the time on the contested votes for arms control and human rights, but less than a quarter of the time on the Middle East. If we were to include the consensus resolutions and count them as votes agreeing with the US position, we

Table 3. General Assembly Voting Coincidence with the United States, 1995–2007, for Issues Resolved not by Consensus but by a Vote (percent)

Year	Arms control	Middle East	Human rights	Overall votes
2007	10.3	11.3	31.9	18.3
2006	29.5	10.7	28.2	23.6
2005	31.7	10.8	35.8	25.0
2004	17.9	9.8	44.9	23.3
2003	30.7	16.5	34.3	25.5
2002	41.9	32.4	23.7	31.2
2001	50.4	29.0	33.9	31.7
2000	66.1	11.9	55.7	43.0
1999	57.9	22.7	52.5	41.8
1998	64.0	22.5	62.8	44.2
1997	65.8	26.2	61.9	46.7
1996	62.3	28.3	68.3	49.4
1995	60.9	35.2	81.0	50.6

Source: US Department of State, *Twenty-fifth Annual Report on Voting Practices in the UN, 2007,* 3 (available at http://www.state.gov/plio/conrpt/vtgprac)

would see a 73.5 percent voting coincidence for 2007. That is much higher than the 18.3 percent for overall votes, but still lower than in previous years, when the range for consensus and consensus votes combined was 85 to 88 percent.

The one trend that leaps from the page is the consistent decline in other nations' voting with the United States in the three areas of high concern to America: arms control, the Middle East, and human rights. The low rates of voting coincidence in issues related to the Middle East and human rights are not too surprising, since the United States has historically taken strong positions that do not always find broad international support. In arms control, however, the United States has often been a leader, for example, in pushing for treaties limiting both the deployment of antimissile systems and the development of nuclear and biological weapons.

Top Ten Countries in Order of Voting Coincidence with
the United States in 2007

Israel	Australia
Palau	Canada
Marshall Islands	United Kingdom
Kiribati	France
Micronesia	Monaco

Looking at the years 1995 to 2007, there is a noticeable bump in
2001, when the degree of voting coincidence takes a decided step
down. Leading up to 2001, the degree of coincidence falls a little each
year, a point here, three points there, year after year. In 2001, the step
down is closer to ten or twelve points. After the step down, the levels
generally resume their slow downward slide, with a few brief excep-
tions, such as votes on arms control in 2005 and 2006.

The State Department also reports annually how individual nations
as well as major blocs and regional groupings voted. For example, the
percentage of voting coincidence with the United States on important
votes by geographic groups from 2002 to 2007 was highest for the
Western Europe and Other Group and lowest for the Asian Group and
the African Group. The Latin American and Caribbean Group and the
Eastern Europe Group fell between the extremes (see fig. 1).

Another way to parse the voting is by political grouping. UN member states belong to various affinity groups, such as ASEAN (Association of South East Asian Nations), OIC (Islamic Conference), and
NATO (North Atlantic Treaty Organization). The State Department
annually examines how these blocs voted on issues that the United
States considers important. Between 2002 and 2007 the European
Union, NATO, and the Nordic Group consistently voted with the
United States on key issues, and the Arab Group, ASEAN, OIC, and
the Nonaligned Movement almost as consistently voted otherwise
(see fig. 2).

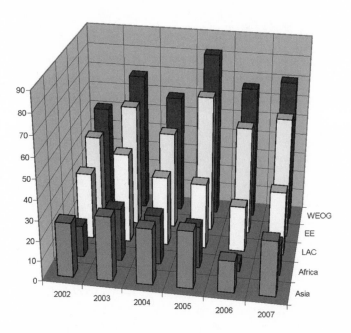

Figure 1. Percentage of voting coincidence with the United States: Important votes by geographic group. *Source:* US Department of State, *Twenty-fifth Annual Report on Voting Practices in the UN, 2007,* 6 (available at www.state .gov/plio/conrpt/vtgprac)

In recent years the number of other nations voting with the United States has generally declined. Even members of NATO, traditional US allies, have been voting with the United States much less since 1995. Western European countries are more likely to vote with the United States than those of other regions, but even they have a lower coincidence than they did in the mid-1990s.

It certainly appears that European nations, which are affluent and developed, are more likely to vote with the United States, whereas developing nations are not. In other words, the North-South divide seems to be in play. The divide's influence may be exacerbated by another factor suggested by insider Jeffrey Laurenti. "Developing

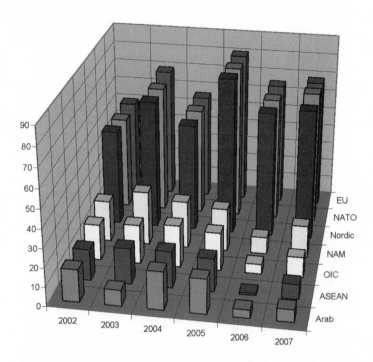

Figure 2. Percentage of voting coincidence with the United States: Important votes by political group. *Source:* US Department of State, *Twenty-fifth Annual Report on Voting Practices in the UN, 2007,* 7 (available at www.state .gov/plio/conrpt/vtgprac)

country democracies do not behave the way Washington does by dint of being democracies, or see things by dint of being democracies," he argues. "The thing that is striking," he continues, "and very hard for many in Washington to understand, including many liberal voices, is that India, South Africa, and Brazil tend to see international crises more like China does than the United States does." Laurenti's explanation for this is that poorer countries "have a different optic than those that are rich and powerful. So they have a tug of claims: the claim of solidarity among the poor of being able to understand things that wealthier countries don't instinctively get, and a sense of doubt about the motivations perhaps of the rich and powerful—in many cases the rich and powerful that have colonized those same countries within living memory."

However we interpret the downward trend in coincidence, we are left with yet another question: What do these numbers mean in terms of American foreign policy? As the State Department's annual report observes, although a nation's UN voting record "is only one dimension of its relations with the U.S.," it is nevertheless a significant factor and "always relevant to its bilateral relationship with the U.S." The report continues that the Security Council and General Assembly are "arguably the most important international bodies in the world, dealing as they do with such vital issues as threats to peace and security, disarmament, development, humanitarian relief, human rights, the environment, and narcotics—all of which can and do directly affect major U.S. interests." The State Department gives copies of its annual report to the foreign ministries and missions of UN member states as a friendly reminder that Uncle Sam is watching.

CHAPTER 9

Peace Operations

What is needed is a streamlined UN decision-making process, ready UN access to military and other forces, and strong investment in diplomacy by key states and institutions. Pressure from NGOs, humanitarian groups, and their supporters will be necessary in order to achieve this sort of systemic change.
—Former US ambassadors Morton Abramowitz and Thomas Pickering

Peace-related issues have always been central to Security Council deliberations, but in the past decade they have become especially numerous and demanding of time and resources. In the 1990s the United Nations launched more peace-related operations than in the previous four decades, and since then the scale of operations has increased. As of mid-2008, seventeen peacekeeping missions and three special missions led by the Department of Peacekeeping Operations employed 109,773 personnel at an annual cost of $6.8 billion. The UN's peacekeepers constitute the second largest deployed military in the world.

The United States has been a strong backer of creating new peacekeeping missions or expanding existing ones—most recently in Leba-

MISSIONS ADMINISTERED BY THE DEPARTMENT OF PEACEKEEPING OPERATIONS

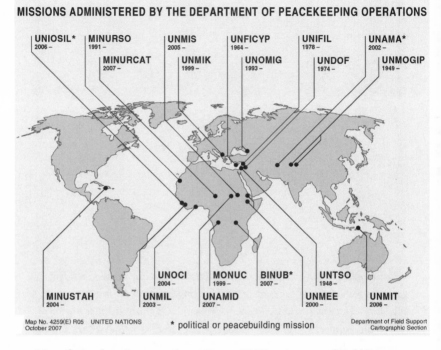

Map of peacekeeping operations. *Source:* UN Department of Field Support, Cartographic Section: 4259(e), April 2008

non, Darfur, Haiti, East Timor, Chad, and the Central African Republic. A recent State Department report noted that the government "supports peacekeeping operations when they can be an effective means of containing conflict and resolving disputes in support of U.S. national interests."

As one of the Permanent Five, the United States can exercise tight control over the whole process, from authorizing a mission to deciding on its size, composition, and level of funding. The United States does not usually provide troops for UN peacekeeping missions, but it is one of the largest financial contributors and is assessed 26 percent of all peacekeeping costs as part of its treaty obligation at the UN.

Once the Security Council authorizes the deployment of an operation, defines its mission, and recommends how it should be carried out, the secretary-general appoints a force commander and, through the Secretariat's Department of Peacekeeping Operations (DPKO), arranges for management and logistics. DPKO was originally one entity, but with the rapid growth of peacekeeping missions in recent years, the General Assembly agreed to split it in two, creating a Department of Field Support (DFS) to look after management and logistics under the supervision of an under-secretary-general. DFS provides expertise and assistance in personnel, budget and finance, communications, information technology, and logistics for peacekeepers scattered around the globe.

Member states are asked to provide personnel, equipment, and logistics. The UN pays member states, per peacekeeper per month, $1,028 for pay and allowances, $303 supplementary pay for specialists, $68 for personal clothing, gear, and equipment, and $5 for personal weaponry. The member states pay the troops according to their own scales and retain control over their units.

The two charts on the next page describe how member states contribute to the peacekeeping effort. The top chart shows that the countries contributing the most uniformed personnel—that is, troops and police—are Pakistan, Bangladesh, India, Nigeria, Nepal, Ghana, Jordan, and Rwanda. The lower chart shows the major financial backers, leading off with numero uno, the United States, and continuing with Japan, Germany, the United Kingdom, France, and Italy. China and Russia contribute about as much as some significantly smaller nations, such as Canada and Greece.

An Evolving Concept

Although peacekeeping is one of the quintessential UN functions, the Charter mentions it only briefly. Its full scope and nature have emerged over the decades in response to pressing needs to help make the peace and keep it. The Security Council's first peacekeeping resolution set important precedents, establishing the United Nations Truce Supervi-

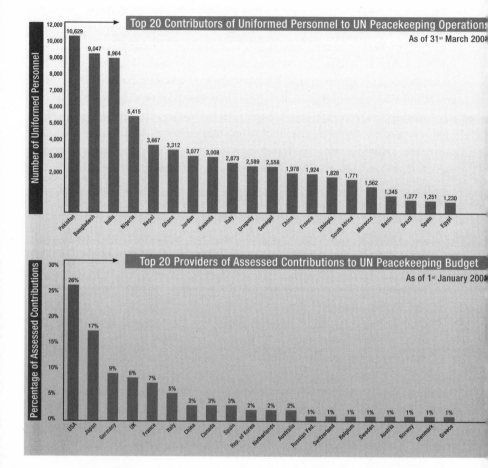

Top contributors of personnel (top) and assessed contributions (bottom) to UN peacekeeping, April 2008. *Source:* UNDPKO and UNDPI, "Fact Sheet, United Nations Peacekeeping," DPI/2429/Rev.2—May 2008

Secretary-General Ban Ki-moon meets with UNTSO staff in Jerusalem, March 27, 2007. UN Photo/Evan Schneider

sion Organization (UNTSO) in 1948 to oversee the truce between Arabs and Jews when the British relinquished control over Palestine. Like peacekeeping today, member states provided the troops, who wore the blue helmets that have marked UN peacekeepers ever since. UNTSO also set the model for nomenclature: the organization is invariably referred to by its acronym rather than its full name. Still in operation, UNTSO has an expanded mandate that includes supervising the implementation and observance of the general agreements between Israel and its four Arab neighbors.

The nature of peacekeeping has changed as the nature of conflicts has evolved. The norm used to be that conflicts occurred between nation-states, which fought with field armies that targeted combatants, not civilians—that was the theory, anyway. For national wars, UN peacekeeping operations have typically consisted of military observers charged with monitoring truces, troop withdrawals, and borders or demilitarized zones. Other operations have involved military forma-

Seal of Approval

In April 2008, Assistant Secretary of State for International Government Affairs Kristen Silverberg stated that the Bush administration "considers United Nations peacekeeping to be in the direct national security interest of the United States. It deserves and it receives both our political and our financial support."
—US Department of State Bureau of International Information Programs

tions capable of acting as buffers between hostile forces. But these days nation-states have been remarkably well behaved toward one another, and in some places, such as Europe, they have even forged close political ties. Instead, conflicts tend to occur within nations, in the form of civil wars (as in Rwanda, Sudan, and the former Yugoslavia) or national resistance movements (such as East Timorese against Indonesian occupation and independence fighters in Kosovo).

For these internal conflicts, UN peacekeeping operations may combine military and police or civilian functions and personnel, with the aim of creating or strengthening political institutions, providing emergency aid, clearing land mines, and administering and monitoring free elections. The presence of police units has become increasingly important, including Formed Police Units, which are more heavily armed than regular UNPOL (United Nations Police) teams and fill the gap between the military component of peacekeeping and the capacity of the local police. Such units helped reestablish government control in gang-infested parts of Haiti in 2007 and helped evacuate civilians caught in gun battles in the Democratic Republic of the Congo.

It is also now widely accepted that peacekeeping forces should include women serving in significant numbers and making meaningful contributions, and so the UN's Department of Peacekeeping Operations is working to increase the number of female peacekeepers in the field. Residents of Liberia's capital, Monrovia, got the first look at peacekeeping's newest face—Formed Police Units consisting of women from

India. Dressed in blue uniforms and toting rifles, the 105 female police officers began patrolling the city streets and enforcing curfews, preventing crime, arresting suspects, and in general ensuring the safety and security of residents.

Peacebuilding Commission

"Peacebuilding" is a term of recent origin that defines UN activities to establish the foundations of peace and provide the tools for building on those foundations. Peacebuilding includes strengthening the rule of law, improving respect for human rights, providing technical assistance for democratic development, and promoting conflict resolution and reconciliation techniques.

The concept went from rhetoric to reality in December 2005, when the General Assembly and the Security Council passed resolutions founding a Peacebuilding Commission. The US government backed creation of the new commission, but John Bolton, who became US ambassador to the UN after it was created, is skeptical that it was needed. "It's not as if the council is not aware that there are economic, social, and other factors in addition to political and military factors that are critical to maintaining a lasting peace in context after context. They don't need a separate commission to do that."

The commission is an intergovernmental advisory body that supports efforts to stabilize and rebuild countries emerging from war. It draws resources from the new UN Peacebuilding Fund (PBF), established in 2006 to "kick-start" postconflict peacebuilding. As of autumn 2007, the fund had received pledges of $230.5 million from thirty-eight member states and had collected $144 million of the pledges. It had begun twenty-four projects, many in Africa. In Sierra Leone, for example, the PBF helped pay the salaries of thirty thousand polling staff during national elections, in addition to funding the purchase of equipment for local police to control disturbances. The new approach tries to engage all stakeholders in dialogue, which means governments, of course, but also nongovernmental organizations and other groups.

A Peace Glossary

Just as Eskimos are said to have many words for snow, the UN has developed an array of words and phrases for the making and keeping of peace. Here are just a few.

preventive diplomacy: As its name suggests, preventive diplomacy seeks to head off disputes before they become full-blown conflicts. The UN prefers this kind of diplomacy but is able to apply it in only some instances. The UN employs its extensive contacts and offices around the world to detect early signs of potential threats to international peace and security.

peacemaking: Peacemaking involves the use of diplomacy to persuade belligerents to stop fighting and negotiate an end to their dispute.

peace enforcement: Peace enforcement involves the use of force against one of the belligerents to enforce an end to the fighting.

peace-building: Peace-building involves helping nations promote peace before, during, or after a conflict. Broadly defined, it employs a wide range of political, humanitarian, and human rights activities and programs.

Another recent innovation is the creation in 2007 of the Office of Rule of Law and Security Institutions (OROLSI), charged with providing an integrated approach to UN assistance in the area of rule of law and security. The secretary-general asked the General Assembly to approve establishment of the office in response to the so-called Brahimi report of 2000, which the Security Council commissioned to suggest improvements to UN peacekeeping operations. The ensuing report, by Lakhdar Brahimi, the former foreign minister of Algeria, is often consulted and cited by proponents of rebuilding or at least remodeling the peacekeeping system. Some have likened UN peacekeeping to a volunteer fire department, but it's not that well organized, according to former secretary-general Kofi Annan, because for every mission it is necessary to scrounge up the fire engines and the money to pay for them "before we can start dousing any flames."

The Brahimi report made many recommendations about updating the concept of peacekeeping to address modern situations and stressed the growing need for better funding and administration. It urged that military functions be integrated with historically civil concerns such as human rights, policing, and food, shelter, and medical services. The rule of law is an important component of such integration—hence the creation of OROLSI. The new office combines many previously scattered UN entities, such as the police division and the judicial, legal, and correctional units. The goal is to develop a "holistic approach" by incorporating all aspects of rule of law and security into a network that includes the police, the judiciary, and corrections, according to its newly appointed director, Dmitry Titov of the Russian Federation.

The Talking Cure

The Security Council has to address so many requests for making or keeping peace that it usually begins by looking for a solution that does not involve the deployment of UN peacekeepers. The Department of Political Affairs is the lead UN department for peacemaking and preventive diplomacy, often working behind the scenes to define and plan the mission and to provide UN special envoys and mediators with guidance and backing from headquarters.

A good example of how the UN tries to resolve issues through discussion is the conflict between Ethiopia and Eritrea, a breakaway province that is now an independent nation and UN member state. The conflict began in the 1990s and has moved haltingly and slowly to resolution, largely through UN and regional efforts. During the early 1980s, Ethiopia, a landlocked country, unilaterally annexed Eritrea, which gave Ethiopia a port on the Red Sea; but the Eritreans resisted and finally secured their independence after a long war. Then, on May 6, 1998, the Eritrean government ordered its armed forces to occupy a slice of disputed territory on the border with Ethiopia. A regional body, the Organization of African Unity (OAU, now the African Union), worked out an agreement for settling the dispute, but neither side would commit to it. In February 1999, the Security Council stepped in and urged the disputants to accept the OAU's plan. When they refused and began fighting, the council moved to its next stage of action, which was to tell the combatants to stop fighting, start talking, and arrange a cease-fire. The United States joined the cease-fire efforts, and in February and March 1999 OAU special envoy Ahmed Ouyahia of Algeria and former US national security adviser Anthony Lake visited Asmara and Addis Ababa. Algeria then brought the two parties together for talks, which broke down.

The fighting had stopped by then but seemed on the verge of resuming when, in April, the council reiterated its demand for a cease-fire and implementation of the OAU's plan. In June, the council again asked the two parties to negotiate, citing a looming humanitarian crisis as drought and unrest threatened massive starvation. The United States sent more than seven hundred thousand metric tons of food assistance to Ethiopia and one hundred thousand tons to Eritrea. A UN Security Council mission to Congo, led by US permanent representative Richard Holbrooke, began shuttle diplomacy during several days early in May, with Holbrooke leaning on both sides not to renew the fighting.

The shuttle talks failed, the mission left, and on May 12, 2000, Ethiopia sent its forces deep into Eritrea. The Security Council passed a resolution demanding an end to military action, but the next day Ethiopia's forces made a major breakthrough and eventually advanced to within sixty miles of the Eritrean capital. Then the Ethiopian government, apparently satisfied that it had acquired a good bargaining position, stated that it was ending the war. Meanwhile, the Security Council passed another resolution, 1298, requiring that member states enforce an arms sales embargo on both combatants. Eritrea then declared that it would move its troops back to the border that existed in May 1998.

As each combatant backed off, the OAU, UN, and other parties arranged for new talks in Algiers, which led to an agreement for a cease-fire. Once the fighting ended, the council created the UN Mission in Ethiopia and Eritrea (UNMEE) and charged it with monitoring the border and ensuring that the cease-fire provisions were honored. The council authorized the mission at a strength of more than 4,200 military and other personnel.

UNMEE's Netherlands and Canadian Battalion hands over peacekeeping duties to the Indian Battalion, June 12, 2001. UN Photo/Jorge Aramburu

By then, Ethiopia and Eritrea had been fighting or at least glaring at each other for more than two years. Why did the council wait so long? The answer is that UN peacekeepers traditionally maintain peace once it is agreed to by the combatants, but they do not generally impose peace through military action. A goal of peacekeeping is to prevent fighting from erupting and to give negotiators a chance to find a resolution to the dispute. And that is what has happened in the Ethiopia-Eritrea conflict. In fall 2000, the OAU envoy and Anthony Lake pursued shuttle diplomacy while members of the Security Council urged the disputants to negotiate a complete solution. At Algiers in December 2000 the two nations signed an accord in the presence of Secretary-General Kofi Annan and Secretary of State Madeleine Albright.

The dispute, however, is still not over. An independent commission defined the border between the two countries in 2002, and although Ethiopia disagreed with the border, it nevertheless declared its willing-

The Size and Cost of Peacekeeping Current Operations,
as of April 2008

Personnel
Total personnel serving in twenty DPKO-led operations: 109,773
Countries contributing military personnel and civilian police: 118
International civilian personnel: 5,222
Local civilian personnel: 12,616
Total number of fatalities in peacekeeping operations since 1948:
   2,468
Financial aspects
Approved budgets, July 1, 2007—June 30, 2008: $6.8 billion
Source: UN Department of Public Information, April 2008

ness to honor it. Implementation of the commission's recommendations, however, has been put on hold while the antagonists accuse
each other of infiltrating troops into a buffer zone that was created
along the border. In addition, Ethiopia has refused to hand over the
town of Badme, which was awarded to Eritrea. In November 2006,
the commission gave the rivals a year to mark their border with stone
columns or risk having it set for them. UNMEE was supposed to
remain deployed until the border between the two nations was demar-
cated and the two governments could establish sufficient dialogue to
ensure that they can peacefully resolve any disagreements or misun-
derstandings that might arise. But the Security Council decided to
terminate the mission in July 2008 because of uncooperative behavior from the antagonists, especially Eritrea.

Meanwhile, the plot thickened owing to charges in a UN report (and
by the United States) that Eritrea has been sending large quantities of
money and arms to al-Qaeda–linked Islamist militants in neighbor-
ing Somalia, despite UN and regional efforts to end the Somalian civil
war. Eritrean officials denied the charges, while American officials
complained that Eritrea was playing a destabilizing role in the Horn of
Africa. The outcome of the Eritrea-Ethiopia border dispute has now
become hostage to larger issues, which may hasten or delay a final

resolution, depending on the willingness of the United States and other major actors to pressure the two governments.

Beyond Just Keeping the Peace

Although traditional peacekeeping of the Ethiopia-Eritrea sort remains important, it is increasingly regarded as an opening move in a process of moving from armed conflict to political dialogue and peace.

One place where the UN has applied a more comprehensive approach toward peacekeeping is East Timor when that region began seeking independence from Indonesia. The Security Council hosted negotiations that led in 1999 to a popular referendum in which the Timorese rejected autonomy within Indonesia and opted for independence. But the council had to authorize a multinational security force after Indonesian-backed militants unleashed a campaign of systematic destruction and violence in response to the Timorese referendum. Many East Timorese were killed, and more than two hundred thousand were forced to flee, most to West Timor.

Acting under Chapter VII of the UN Charter, the Security Council established the UN Transitional Administration in East Timor (UNTAET) in 1999 to restore order and provide administrative services as East Timor prepared for independence. Sérgio Vieira de Mello of Brazil was appointed the Transitional Administrator for East Timor. UNTAET began a program of "Timorization" of key government posts to prepare for transition to full independence. In July UNTAET established the East Timor Transitional Administration, with a cabinet of nine ministries, five headed by East Timorese. Then UNTAET appointed a thirty-six-member national council representing a wide spectrum of Timorese society. UNTAET began preparations for elections in late summer 2001 for a national assembly, which drew up and adopted a constitution. In 2002 the Timorese elected a president and became a new nation, Timor-Leste. The new country remains fragile, however, and still requires the presence of UN police units to control civil disturbances. The units are part of a new peacekeeping mission, UNMIT, established in 2006.

The UN's nation-building efforts launched East Timor on its new

A UN police officer discusses security situation with residents of East Timor before the presidential election, May 5, 2007. UN Photo/Martine Perret

path, but interestingly the endeavor got mixed reviews. David Malone praises Vieira de Mello, who "pulled off the East Timor operation in spite of tremendous problems on the ground and enormous bureaucratic inertia within the UN." UN analyst Shepard Forman acknowledges that the effort went fairly well but questions whether it was appropriate: "The UN is questionable as a government in Kosovo and East Timor. Few of the people that went out to govern had any more experience than any of the East Timorese. That's an example of where it [the UN] took on a role to prove itself, and it did an all right job, but we lost a year or so in terms of the Timoreses' own capacity to develop, to reconstruct."

Good, bad, or inappropriate, the complicated and evolving mission to East Timor shows the UN's desire to find new ways of resolving difficult problems—an attribute that is essential if the world body is to adapt and remain vital.

UN Peacekeeping Operations, as of April 2008

UNTSO since May 1948
UN Truce Supervision Organization
Strength: military, 152; international civilians, 106; local civilians, 119
Fatalities: 49
Appropriation 2008–9: $66.2 million

UNMOGIP since January 1949
UN Military Observer Group in India and Pakistan
Strength: military, 44; international civilians, 25; local civilians, 48
Fatalities: 11
Appropriation 2008–9: $16.9 million

UNFICYP since March 1964
UN Peacekeeping Force in Cyprus
Strength: military, 872; police, 66; international civilians, 37; local
 civilians, 108
Fatalities: 177
Approved budget: $48.1 million

UNDOF since June 1974
UN Disengagement Observer Force
Strength: military, 1,047; international civilians, 38; local civilians, 102
Fatalities: 43
Approved budget: $39.7 million

UNIFIL since March 1978
UN Interim Force in Lebanon
Strength: military, 12,341; international civilians, 304; local civilians,
 604
Fatalities: 266
Approved budget: $713.6 million

MINURSO since April 1991
UN Mission for the Referendum in Western Sahara
Strength: military, 20; military observers, 194; police, 6; international
 civilians, 99; local civilians, 148; UN volunteers, 24
Fatalities: 15
Approved budget: $47.6 million

UNOMIG since August 1993
UN Observer Mission in Georgia
Strength: military observers, 134; police, 18; international civilians, 99; local civilians, 183; UN volunteers, 1
Fatalities: 11
Approved budget: $35 million

UNMIK since June 1999
UN Interim Administration Mission in Kosovo
Strength: military observers, 40; police, 1,953; international civilians, 472; local civilians, 1,940; UN volunteers, 132
Fatalities: 53
Approved budget: $210.7 million

MONUC since November 1999
UN Organization Mission in the Democratic Republic of the Congo
Strength: military, 16,649; military observers, 710; police, 1,049; international civilians, 942; local civilians, 2,079; UN volunteers, 571
Fatalities: 123
Approved budget: $1,115.7 million

UNMEE since July 2000
UN Mission in Ethiopia and Eritrea
Strength: military, 407; military observers, 96; international civilians, 146; local civilians, 197; UN volunteers, 63
Fatalities: 20
Approved budget: $113.5 million

UNMIL since September 2003
United Nations Mission in Liberia
Strength: military, 12,242; military observers, 196; police, 1,148; international civilians, 513; local civilians, 940; UN volunteers, 238
Fatalities: 108
Approved budget: $688.4 million

UNOCI since April 2004
United Nations Operation in Côte d'Ivoire
Strength: military, 7,841; military observers, 193; police, 1,182; international civilians, 415; local civilians, 574; UN volunteers, 284
Fatalities: 40
Approved budget: $470.9 million

MINUSTAH since June 2004
United Nations Stabilization Mission in Haiti
Strength: military, 7,064; police, 1,923; international civilians, 511; local civilians, 1,152; UN volunteers, 199
Fatalities: 34
Approved budget: $535.4 million
UNMIS since March 2005
United Nations Mission in the Sudan
Strength: military, 8,714; military observers, 574; police, 664; international civilians, 854; local civilians, 2,342; UN volunteers, 250
Fatalities: 35
Approved budget: $846.3 million
UNMIT since August 2006
United Nations Integrated Mission in Timor-Leste
Strength: military observers, 33; police, 1,546; international civilian, 340; local civilians, 794; UN volunteers, 124
Fatalities: 3
Approved budget: $153.2 million
UNAMID since July 2007
United Nations Integrated Mission in Darfur
Strength: military, 7,372; military observers, 137; police, 1,704; international civilians, 254; local civilians, 706; UN volunteers, 129
Fatalities: 1
Approved budget: $1,275.7 million
MINURCAT since September 2007
United Nations Mission in the Central African Republic and Chad
Strength: military observers, 21; police, 84; international civilians, 48; local civilians, 31; UN volunteers, 22
Fatalities: 0
Approved budget: $182.44 million

In addition, DPKO's responsibilities include three missions:
UNAMA since March 2002
United Nations Assistance Mission in Afghanistan
Strength: military observers, 14; police, 3; international civilians, 205; local civilians, 957; UN volunteers, 25

UNIOSIL since January 2006
United Nations Integrated Office in Sierra Leone
Strength: military observers, 15; police, 27; international civilians, 73;
local civilians, 193; UN volunteers, 40
BINUB since January 2007
United Nations Integrated Office in Burundi
Strength: military observers, 4; police, 11; international civilians, 77;
local civilians, 164; UN volunteers, 58
Source: Adapted from "Current Peacekeeping Operations," DPI/1634/
Rev.82—April 2008, and "United Nations Political and Peacebuilding
Missions, 30 June 2007," http://www.un.org/Depts/dpko/dpko/index
.asp

Producing Results

The UN's peacekeeping operations have had mixed results. Some
have not fulfilled their mission, such as the one in Ethiopia-Eritrea,
which had to be terminated. Others, such as the mission in Western
Sahara (MINURSO), have neither succeeded nor failed but go on
indefinitely with no solution in sight. This is probably one of the
examples that former US ambassador John Bolton has in mind when
he complains about missions that "seem to have gained a degree of
immortality," to the extent that they become part of the landscape and
may even perpetuate the conflict because the parties can avoid having
to negotiate a settlement. "The general problem," he says, is to know
when to start a peacekeeping operation and how to finish it. "The
Security Council really doesn't fulfill its role, and . . . you're not resolving the underlying dispute but yet you're keeping the peacekeeping
operation in the field." Former Ambassador Zalmay Khalilzad, who
succeeded Bolton as permanent representative, offered a similar analysis when he declared that peacekeeping should not be a substitute for
ending conflict. Noting that funds have always been tight, he urged
the UN to organize its efforts more cost-effectively. "While we understand the risks of leaving too soon, we should look to terminate non-
viable peacekeeping operations," he said in April 2008.

True enough, yet against the open-ended and sometimes ineffectual missions, one should weigh those that have succeeded. Both Sierra Leone and Liberia are becoming whole countries again after horrific civil wars, thanks in part to the presence of peacekeeping operations. The UN can also be credited with a willingness to try new models of peacekeeping, such as the hybrid operation that is attempting to bring security to Darfur. There, a complicated internal conflict involving the central government and rebel militias has produced death, misery, and destruction throughout an area larger than France. The standard UN peacekeeping operation consists solely of UN forces, but the government of Sudan has refused to accept such a mission. The UN has therefore partnered with the African Union to deploy a joint peacekeeping force consisting of military units from both organizations. It would be the largest peacekeeping mission ever deployed under the UN banner, if it were permitted to be deployed. At its full authorized strength, UNAMID (United Nations–African Union Mission in Darfur) will deploy nearly twenty thousand troops and more than six thousand police. Ideally, this force will establish a secure environment while talks achieve a lasting civil and political settlement.

Further, though perhaps its efforts should have come earlier, the UN is now trying to address an abuse that has plagued peacekeeping missions for a long time: allegations that some troops have sexually exploited civilians. These accusations have become more common as the scale of peacekeeping has grown. In 2006, for example, there were 357 allegations of sexual exploitation and abuse involving UN peacekeepers, and 252 were substantial enough to warrant investigation.

The growing caseload led to calls for a renewed commitment to investigate and prosecute those accused and to help the victims. Both the General Assembly and the Secretariat have given sexual abuse issues a high priority. All personnel deployed in peacekeeping have received DPKO training on the prevention of sexual exploitation and abuse, and troop-contributing countries are urged to cooperate in investigating allegations of wrongdoing. In 2006 the director of DPKO, Jean-Marie Guéhenno of France, briefed the Security Council on his efforts to make troop-contributing countries more sensitive to sexual abuse. In 2007 the General Assembly adopted a strategy on

Assistance and Support to Victims of Sexual Exploitation and Abuse by UN staff and related personnel, and in 2008 Secretary-General Ban Ki-moon said he was planning to launch "a major initiative" to curb violence against "women around the world." These efforts are offered as one reason for a sharp decline in sexual abuse accusations in at least one peacekeeping operation, in Liberia, in 2007. If the UN can leverage this success into a broader improvement across its operations, it will have made an important advance both in peacekeeping and in human rights.

Outside observers are generally impressed with the effectiveness of peacekeeping operations and their larger significance for making the world a safer place. The *Human Security Report*, an international study published in 2005, cited UN peacekeeping efforts as one factor in the striking improvement in the world's security between 1988 and 2001. The American government has also praised UN peacekeeping. The Government Accountability Office estimates that UN peacekeeping, on average, is at least eight times cheaper than having the United States undertake its own peacekeeping operations. The White House Office of Management and Budget recently gave the US contributions to UN peacekeeping its highest possible rating and assessed the fiscal cost to be effective in achieving its stated goals and in contributing to American objectives.

CHAPTER 10

Stopping International
Terrorism and WMD Proliferation

There is no more urgent threat to the United States than a terrorist with a nuclear weapon. Nuclear weapons materials are stored in dozens of countries, some without proper security. Nuclear technology is spreading. . . . It is essential to strengthen the global nonproliferation and disarmament regime, dealing with those states in violation of this regime, and upholding our obligations to work constructively and securely toward the goal of a world without nuclear weapons.

—Susan E. Rice, US ambassador to the UN

On the day after 9/11, the Security Council officially decreed that acts of international terrorism are threats to international peace and security. The events of September 11 also pushed the council to act quickly in creating a broad resolution aimed at cutting off all support to international terrorists. "The UN rewrote the law after the 9/11 attacks by stating that countries have an affirmative duty not to give any kind of assistance to terrorist groups [Resolution 1373]," remarks international law expert Ruth Wedgwood of Johns Hopkins University. "It changed the terms of state responsibility. It was a hugely important resolution."

The shocking attacks of September 11 placed the United States at the top of the list of terror-afflicted nations and helped raise international awareness about the urgency of the threat. The media were filled with stories and editorials about the need to find terrorists and neutralize them before they could mount another major attack, possibly one using weapons of mass destruction, or WMDs.

One immediate response by the United States and many of its friends was to treat terrorism as a variety of military threat, to be countered with the use of force, as in Afghanistan, where al-Qaeda had formed a close alliance with the Taliban government and was using its resources to train recruits. The United States soon launched an invasion, with UN approval, that overthrew the Taliban regime and forced al-Qaeda into hiding.

Another response, not only by the United States and its friends but also by the UN, was to treat international terrorism as a form of criminal activity that needs to be made clearly illegal everywhere, both within nations and in international law. As the world's global forum, the UN is ideally suited for this task. The UN has defined several important counterterrorism roles for itself, such as norm-setting, observes Pakistan's ambassador Munir Akram: "Setting up international public opinion, standards, and conventions which have outlawed terrorism and made it possible for countries to cooperate with each other on concrete terms."

An Emerging Consensus

A striking aspect of recent counterterrorist deliberations is that the major powers all seem to be generally on the same page. The Security Council's Permanent Five publicly and officially agree that only through joint efforts can they hope to stop or reduce terrorism. They have expressed their unity through a series of resolutions, beginning in late 1999, when the Security Council passed a resolution requiring the Taliban government in Afghanistan to give up Osama bin Laden, whose al-Qaeda network had been targeting US government and military facilities. Next, Resolution 1269 pledged a "common fight against terrorists everywhere" and specified that member states should share information and refuse to provide a safe haven to terrorists. At the end of 1999, the General Assembly voted to adopt the International Convention for the Suppression of the Financing of Terrorism. This convention makes it a crime to participate in raising funds for terrorist activity, even if no terrorist act ensues.

Then came 9/11. Security Council Resolution 1373, approved on September 28, 2001, requires every UN member state to freeze the financial assets of terrorists and their supporters, deny them travel or safe haven, prevent terrorist recruitment and weapons supply, and cooperate with other countries in information sharing and criminal prosecution.

Resolution 1373 also established the Counter-Terrorism Committee (CTC), which aims to strengthen the capacity of UN member states and coordinate the counterterrorism efforts of regional and intergovernmental organizations both inside and outside the UN system. In 2004 the council adopted Resolution 1535, which created the Counter Terrorism Executive Directorate, designed to give the CTC greater technical capability and expand its ability to help member states implement the provisions of Resolution 1373.

One of the CTC's greatest contributions has been to amass information about the ability of UN member states to fight terrorism. "Of course, the hard work against terrorism on the ground is done by national governments or international agencies," says Ambassador Akram, and therefore these governments are the focus of the CTC's activities. Under Resolution 1373, each member state must submit an annual report on its antiterrorism activities and capabilities.

Many member states have submitted the required annual reports, giving the CTC extensive data about the antiterrorism capacity in each nation. But the annual reports have revealed that many of the smaller or less developed nations lack key elements of an effective strategy. Most of these states do not have the legal, administrative, and regulatory capabilities to freeze financial assets, deny safe haven to terrorists, or prevent terrorism groups from recruiting new members and acquiring weapons.

Terrorism and Failed States

"An area where we do spend a lot of our time is the issue of failed states. The breeding ground for terrorism or proliferation or any other manner of ills of this world, whether it's narcotics trafficking or other forms of antisocial behavior, is more likely to develop in a country whose institutions have broken down. . . . That's what Osama bin Laden did when he moved in on the Taliban and used Afghanistan for his own purposes. We at the UN have an interest in states not failing and we spend a lot of time dealing with states that are threatened in that way."
—John Negroponte, former US ambassador to the UN

The CTC has tried to help these nations get the technical expertise needed to upgrade their capability, but so far the demand for assistance has outpaced the ability to provide it. Efforts are also hindered by the CTC's decision not to sit in judgment of UN member states or to report noncomplying governments to the Security Council. The CTC has taken this stance to maintain engagement with all member states rather than risk alienating them by being too aggressive in providing assistance to encouraging compliance. The flip side of engagement, however, is that the committee allows certain countries to avoid responsibility for taking specific action.

The Debate over Solutions

Another barrier to full implementation of Resolution 1373 is the lack of consensus over which possible lines of action are most likely to eliminate terrorism. In part this derives from an inability of all nations to agree on a clear and generally accepted definition of terrorism. The General Assembly has been deliberating on counterterrorism measures to augment the thirteen international conventions now on the books. As you might expect, the assembly's diverse membership has struggled to find consensus, especially on the question of a definition.

Even the much smaller Security Council has been unable to agree on a clear definition. To cite one instance, in a recent Security Council meeting, those delegates who stated a position on the matter had differing views on the desirability of defining terrorism. The Libyan delegate thought that there was need for a "clear" definition. The representative from India thought that "there was no need for a philosophical definition of terrorism" because the UN already had plenty of language making terrorism a criminal activity. The representative of Venezuela thought that "in the short run, it was important to create a definition of terrorism," but it should not be equated with "legitimate struggles for national liberty and self-determination by people under colonial or foreign occupation." However, the United States and its friends refuse to accept the sort of distinction made by the Venezuelan representative.

Former US ambassador John Bolton has a criticism about such debates: "The conclusion you have to draw from the record on terrorism," he says, "where the Security Council creates a committee on terrorism but can't even agree on a definition of what terrorism is . . . is that it's not going to be effective in those areas."

Pakistan's Munir Akram is just as impatient with the debates about finding a definition of terrorism, but for quite different reasons. "Perhaps the search for a definition of terrorism is a red herring," he argues. "We all know what terrorism is when we see it, and therefore the search for a legal definition perhaps is not the most urgent effort." Rather, he maintains, it is more important to understand that terrorism takes many forms, different from place to place. "We have to address it globally, but we have to act locally." Further, Akram claims, "a practical, pragmatic approach—which is not set in ideology," has the best chance of succeeding. We should say, he continues, "No, these are not terrorists because they are Islamists. No, an Islamist or a Christian or a Jewish person doing terrorism cannot be defined by his religion, he is defined by his motivations." And these motivations may vary: "If you dig deeply into his motivations you would find they are largely political, and at times economic, and at times societal, and at times they are spiritual. One needs to understand the motivations of these people who are attracted to terrorism and try to address them. That's the only way in which we can have a long-term solution to the problem of terrorism."

The Threat of Weapons of Mass Destruction

Much of the urgency for acting against terrorism comes from the fear that a terrorist group might acquire WMDs, such as poisonous chemicals, deadly microorganisms, or radioactive or even fissile material that could cause harm on a scale far beyond what happened on 9/11. When the Soviet Union imploded in the early 1990s, some experts warned about the danger of unauthorized access to nuclear weapons or nuclear materials such as enriched uranium. In the aftermath of September 11, the UN's International Atomic Energy Agency (IAEA) has led the conversation about preventing terrorists from using nuclear weapons. It is the world's forum for discussing, debating, and regulating the peaceful, and sometimes not so peaceful, use of atomic energy. Mohamed ElBaradei, IAEA director from 1999 to 2009, has noted that because terrorists are willing to take their own lives when committing their violence, the nuclear threat is very serious. The IAEA operates the Emergency Response Center, the world's only international response system capable of reacting quickly to the effects of a nuclear terrorist attack. Between 1993 and 2004, the IAEA identified 220 cases of trafficking in nuclear material, of which only eighteen involved highly enriched uranium or plutonium.

Nevertheless, the threat remains as long as national governments maintain stockpiles of nuclear weapons and weapons-grade uranium. This came home in 2004, when it was discovered that a Pakistani nuclear scientist, A. Q. Khan, who had helped develop his nation's nuclear bomb, had sold sensitive information to North Korea. It is not hard to imagine someone else, likewise well placed in a national atomic weapons program, offering to sell similar information to a terrorist organization.

The need to address this potential threat has elicited two types of reply. One says that the solution is to get rid of all nuclear weapons, so that no one, including terrorists, would have access to the information and technology necessary for building a bomb. The other approach accepts the need for some nations to have nuclear weapons and places the emphasis on ensuring that no other countries develop their own. The United States and other nuclear powers generally prefer this so-called antiproliferation argument, while many nonnuclear and developing nations prefer to abolish atomic bombs and weapons entirely.

One of Kofi Annan's last speeches as secretary-general dealt with precisely this dilemma. He began with the Nuclear Non-Proliferation Treaty of 1970, which the Soviet Union and the United States signed as part of a joint effort to limit the spread of nuclear weapons beyond the few great powers that possessed them at the time. Annan characterized the treaty as "a contract" between the nuclear states and the rest of the world. The nuclear states declared that they would negotiate in good faith on nuclear disarmament, prevent proliferation, and encourage the peaceful use of nuclear energy. In return, noted Annan, the nonnuclear nations agreed not to acquire or manufacture nuclear weapons and to place all their nuclear activities under the verification of the IAEA.

The stability engendered by the agreement lasted until the 1990s, Annan continued, when problems arose about how to interpret and implement the treaty. The international community was unable to agree how to apply the treaty to specific crises in the Korean peninsula and the Middle East, and a few states that had ratified the treaty were accused of trying to develop nuclear weapons.

The debate about the treaty had become deadlocked between two seemingly irreconcilable viewpoints, noted Annan. The "nonproliferation first" advocates, mainly nuclear-weapon states and their supporters, saw the main danger arising, "not from nuclear weapons as such, but from the character of those who possess them, and therefore from the spread of nuclear weapons to new states and to non-state actors." On the other side, "disarmament first" advocates saw nuclear arsenals and their continual improvement as the source of danger. They complained that "the UN Security Council has often described the proliferation of weapons of mass destruction as a threat to interna-

Thirteen Counterterrorism Conventions and Protocols

The UN has thirteen antiterrorism conventions and protocols:

1. Convention on Offenses and Certain Other Acts Committed on Board Aircraft, 1963 (Tokyo Convention)
2. Convention for the Suppression of the Unlawful Seizure of Aircraft, 1970 (Hague Convention)
3. Convention for the Suppression of Unlawful Acts against the Safety of Civil Aviation, 1971 (Montreal Convention)
4. Convention on the Prevention and Punishment of Crimes against Internationally Protected Persons, 1973
5. International Convention against the Taking of Hostages, 1979 (Hostages Convention)
6. Convention on the Physical Protection of Nuclear Material, 1980
7. Protocol for the Suppression of Unlawful Acts of Violence at Airports Serving International Civil Aviation, 1988, supplementary to the Convention for the Suppression of Unlawful Acts against the Safety of Civil Aviation
8. Convention for the Suppression of Unlawful Acts against the Safety of Maritime Navigation, 1988
9. Protocol for the Suppression of Unlawful Acts against the Safety of Fixed Platforms Located on the Continental Shelf, 1988
10. Convention on the Marking of Plastic Explosives for the Purpose of Detection, 1991
11. International Convention for the Suppression of Terrorist Bombings, 1997
12. International Convention for the Suppression of the Financing of Terrorism, 1999
13. International Convention for the Suppression of Acts of Nuclear Terrorism, 2005

UN offices in Algiers destroyed by a terrorist bombing, December 11, 2007. UN Photo/Evan Schneider

tional peace and security, but has never declared that nuclear weapons
in and of themselves are such a threat."

Annan urged the UN and the world community to push for both
nonproliferation and disarmament, as two halves of a complete solution, but his argument has not led to decisive action. So far, the Security Council has retained an antiproliferation stance. For example,
when pressed to make a formal declaration about reining in weapons
of mass destruction, it chose the antiproliferation perspective. Resolu-

tion 1540, passed in 2004, marks an important international attempt to limit weapons of mass destruction and related materials in an integrated and comprehensive manner. The resolution highlights the growing threat posed by WMD proliferation to international security. It is aimed at preventing the proliferation of nuclear, chemical, and biological weapons to both states and nonstate groups.

Aside from weapons programs, civilian nuclear power programs offer another potential source of enriched uranium, either for processing into a fission bomb or for use as a "dirty" bomb that produces massive radiation. The more these civilian programs expand, the greater is the risk of proliferation, especially in nations with lesser political stability. Ruth Wedgwood calls this "a fatal flaw" in the Nuclear Non-Proliferation Treaty: "The assumption was that you could segregate civilian and military uses. . . . But enriched uranium is enriched uranium, as North Korea and Iran have shown. The irony is that if you have the proliferation of civilian uses, you're going to have proliferation of weapons uses."

Can the UN Do It?

As UN resolutions on terrorism have followed, one after the other, there is a growing sentiment among some experts that the organization's reach may be exceeding its grasp. It is fine to outlaw terrorist acts, they note, but quite another thing to get compliance from member states. Moreover, antiterrorism often requires exactly the kind of stealthy intelligence gathering and quick action that the UN is not known for. According to William Luers, "Certain issues in global affairs the UN is not equipped to deal with, such as international terrorism, illicit trafficking in humans, and drugs, all flowing out of globalization." The UN, he argues, "has not faced up to terrorism. It has committees and great intentions, but the nature of terrorism doesn't allow for a decisive UN role, though it is seeking to identify what that might be."

Indeed, the UN is itself becoming a target of terrorists. In December 2007, an al-Qaeda–inspired suicide bombing destroyed the UN headquarters building in Algiers and killed nearly forty people, including seventeen UN employees. Al-Qaeda and its affiliates have also threatened or targeted UN officials and peacekeepers in Afghanistan, Iraq, Somalia, Sudan, and southern Lebanon. The head of a UN team that monitors the effectiveness of UN sanctions against al-Qaeda and the Taliban has stated that "al-Qaeda certainly regards the UN as inimical to its own interests." One of the UN's longtime troubleshooters, Lakhdar Brahimi, was appointed the head of a panel to review security at the organization's facilities worldwide. "I think there are quite a lot of people who do not make a secret that they consider that the UN has become their enemy," he told reporters. "I think the UN has been put on notice that their flag is not anymore a protection," Brahimi said ominously.

Despite the UN's limitations and vulnerabilities, it does provide access to important information for the counterterrorism effort, and it has a significant coordinating function as well. Ambassador Akram puts it this way: "The UN is important because it maintains the international consensus on the issue of terrorism, how to address terrorism and try to take into account the views and interests of all concerned." In the long term, the UN's greatest contribution may include its social and economic programs, which Akram sees as addressing the root causes of terrorism. "The major focus has to be on economic and social development, on education, on efforts to wean away the appeal of terrorism."

CHAPTER 11

Climate Change

To tackle global warming, all major emitting nations must be part of the solution, and rapidly developing economies, such as China and India, must join in making and meeting their own binding and meaningful commitments. We must help the most vulnerable countries adapt to climate change and seize opportunities to accelerate their development by investing in supplying renewable energy and participating in emissions trading mechanisms.

—Susan E. Rice, US ambassador to the UN

We all know the saying, People talk about the weather but no one does anything about it. That's only partly true nowadays. Not only do we talk about the weather, especially that part of it called global warming, but we are even trying to do something about it. And the UN is in the middle of the whole effort.

Talk about climate change has been around for more than half a century, when scientists began debating a theory that modern industrial society is capable of transforming the weather through its rising emissions of so-called greenhouse gases. Carbon dioxide and methane are among the gases that have a curious property: like the glass panes in a greenhouse, they are barriers to the radiation of heat. When humans burn carbon-based fuels and increase the level of heat in the vast greenhouse we call the atmosphere, they also raise the level of greenhouse gases. These gases trap more of the heat instead of letting it radiate into outer space, and over time the atmosphere becomes noticeably warmer. Eventually, the theory goes, atmospheric temperatures will rise enough to start changing weather patterns.

Global climate change through human action remained a provocative but obscure theory until the 1980s, when scientists began developing sensing mechanisms and computer programs sophisticated enough to begin tracking worldwide temperature changes and analyzing how the warming might someday play out in real-time weather. Mounting evidence was so persuasive that by the new millennium most scientists accepted some kind of link between rising global temperatures and the emission of greenhouse gases.

Establishing the Facts

One of the most influential groups in this emerging discussion was the UN Intergovernmental Panel on Climate Change (IPCC). Established in 1988 by the UN Environmental Programme and another UN-related body, the World Meteorological Organization, the IPCC began to review the world's scientific literature to make an impartial assessment of human impacts on the climate. Its official reports, issued in 1990, 1995, 2001, and 2008, are now seen as decisive factors in changing how the world thinks about climate change.

In sober and carefully reasoned prose, the IPCC's reports have laid out the facts—based on the research and analysis of thousands of scientists worldwide—and have concluded that human activity is indeed changing the climate and will continue to do so if current conditions persist. For its impressive work, the IPCC was awarded the 2007 Nobel Peace Prize jointly with noted environmental activist, writer, and former US vice president Al Gore.

As the case for global warming shaped up, experts began asking the next two key questions: Is this a totally bad thing? And if so, what can we do to stop it or reverse it?

The consensus position today is that on balance continued global

The General Assembly panel on climate change, February 11, 2008. UN Photo/Jenny Rockett

warming would disrupt many aspects of life and possibly bring social and economic upheaval. It is clear, for example, that a warmer earth would cause the melting of glaciers and polar ice sheets, causing the sea to rise. Coastal cities like Shanghai, New York, and Mumbai and low-lying island nations might then have to plan for a very wet future. Other effects would seem likely, too, such as the drying out of the American Midwest, which might be extreme enough to end large-scale agriculture in the famous Corn Belt. Alongside the losers there would probably be some winners, as clouds moved to new latitudes and brought rain to today's deserts, but these improvements would be small compared to the harm suffered in densely populated regions.

Mobilizing the Response

Fortunately, the UN has already begun organizing the world's governments to curb the emission of greenhouse gases. The first steps were two UN-sponsored meetings, the so-called Earth Summit of 1992 and the Kyoto Protocol of 1997.

The 1992 Conference on Environment and Development, commonly known as the Earth Summit, met in Rio de Janeiro and adopted Agenda 21, a plan for global sustainable development that is being monitored by a UN body, the Commission on Sustainable Development. Five years after the summit, the General Assembly held a special session, Earth Summit +5, to assess progress (which was very uneven) and suggest further action.

The Kyoto Protocol addresses global warming caused by human action. Delegates at the Earth Summit had been given the opportunity to sign the UN Framework Convention on Climate Change (1992), which urged industrialized nations to reduce their emission of greenhouse gases to 1990 levels by 2000. The need for action was then documented, in 1995, in a report by the IPCC. Despite mounting evidence of climate change, some highly developed nations such as the United States refused to comply with the 1992 framework, claiming potential loss of economic growth.

To push matters along, the UN sponsored a meeting in Kyoto, Japan, in December 1997, where major industrialized nations signed a protocol setting hard-and-fast targets for decreasing the emission of six greenhouse gases by more than 5 percent by 2012. Developing nations were exempted from the reduction target, although the largest of them, China, became the world's biggest emitter of carbon dioxide in 2006.

Ban Ki-moon sees America as a key player in the effort. In July 2007, he urged the United States to lead the effort against global warming, declaring that "the whole planet Earth is at a crucial juncture." The cost of inaction "will be far greater than the cost of action," he said. While noting that the UN accepted responsibility for helping to muster the political will to address climate change, he argued that the United States was "in the best position to bring change" because of its advanced technology and its status as one of the largest producers of greenhouse gasses. He declared, "If you take leadership, I think we can save this planet earth from plunging into a very difficult situation.

Updating Kyoto

While the United States, China, and other nations weigh their options, the secretary-general has pushed ahead forcefully to make climate change a key part of his agenda. In December 2007, he spoke at the UN climate change summit in Bali, where representatives from 163 nations agreed to devise a new emissions-cutting plan, by the end of 2009, that would supplant the Kyoto Protocol. This is a difficult negotiation, pitting rich against poor, developed against developing nations. National governments now accept the reality of global warming from greenhouse gases, but they differ on how to fix the problem. The Europeans have proposed that the industrialized nations slash their emissions sharply, but the United States and China, which are the largest emitters of greenhouse gases, have resisted the imposition of formal emissions caps. After Bali, the delegates resumed the debate in Bangkok, in spring 2008, and many more meetings are planned to hammer out a final plan and document.

Meanwhile, Ban Ki-moon has been using his bully pulpit to rally key sectors of the economy to go "green" in their thinking. For example, in 2008, he addressed some 450 participants at the General Assembly's Third Annual Summit on Climate Risk. "Climate change is your opportunity to invest in new kinds of cleaner technologies, industries and jobs," he told the attending financiers, financial managers, and business leaders. "While the world looks to the United Nations to steward the negotiating process [on emissions curbs], the United Nations looks to you, as leaders in the financial sector, to lead in innovative financing and technological development."

The secretary-general places a lot of importance on getting the business and financial sectors behind the climate change issue. "I'm encouraging businesses to get involved," Ban said recently. "With the private sector's well-known ingenuity harnessed in the battle against climate change, we can leverage costs into economic gain. That's good corporate citizenship—but it also makes sound economic sense. I've personally met with business leaders in major cities across the United States and elsewhere to drive home this point."

Secretary-General Ban Ki-moon in Antarctica, November 9, 2007. UN
Photo/Eskinder Debebe

Ban Ki-moon's strategy has been to engage a wide range of stakeholders in the discussion because he believes that climate change is
everyone's concern. The UN is ideally suited to this kind of global
consensus building. If penguins and polar bears could speak, they
would probably join the debate.

CHAPTER 12

The Rule of Law and Human Rights

*And so when we respect our international legal obligations and support an
international system based on the rule of law, we do the work of making the
world a better place, but also a safer and more secure place for America.*
— Former US secretary of state Condoleeza Rice

Rights come first everywhere you look at the United Nations. The
purpose of the organization, according to Article 1 of the Charter, is to
promote and encourage "respect for human rights and for fundamental freedoms for all without distinction as to race, sex, language, or
religion." The Universal Declaration of Human Rights, as we saw
earlier, is literally all about rights (see appendix B). Nearly all states
that join the UN have agreed to accept its principles by signing and
ratifying two international covenants, one addressing civil and political rights and the other economic, social, and cultural rights. The
International Covenant on Civil and Political Rights and the International Covenant on Economic, Social, and Cultural Rights, which entered force in 1976, are legally binding documents. When combined
with the Universal Declaration, they constitute the International Bill
of Human Rights.

The assistant secretary-general for the rule of law addresses the Security Council, May 7, 2008. UN Photo/Devra Berkowitz

An Emerging Body of Law

Having rights, real ones that you can actually use, requires more than rhetoric and fancy legal language, however. Rights imply the rule of law, based on the notion that all citizens are equal before the law and that the law will be applied in a rational, consistent manner. You also need mechanisms for protecting and enforcing both laws and the exercise of rights. All of these things are represented in the UN's law and rights establishment, ranging from national tribunals to international courts, and including a council and executive dedicated to rights issues. It's hardly surprising, though, that legal and rights issues have raised considerable controversy in the UN during the past half-century or that the world body's ability to deliver on its promises has varied greatly.

The UN is justifiably proud of having helped create a large body of human rights law during the past half-century. Most member states have signed and ratified some eighty treaties (also called conventions or covenants) that cover particular aspects of human rights. The International Law Commission is the body that does the actual drafting of text for international conventions. Here are only a few, with their initiation dates:

1948 Convention on the Prevention and Punishment of the Crime of Genocide

1961 Convention Relating to the Status of Refugees

1965 International Convention on the Elimination of All Forms of Racial Discrimination

1984 Convention against Torture and Other Cruel, Inhuman, or Degrading Treatment or Punishment

1990 International Convention on the Protection of the Rights of All Migrant Workers and Members of Their Families

When a convention enters force, the UN may create a watchdog committee charged with ensuring that its provisions are honored by member states. For example, when the Convention on the Rights of the Child entered force in 1989, it was accompanied by the creation of the Committee on the Rights of the Child, which meets regularly and has become an international voice for children.

All offices and staff of the UN and its peacekeeping operations are responsible for adhering to international human rights law and reporting possible breaches of it to the proper authorities. The UN regards human rights as so important that it designated ten years as the UN Decade for Human Rights Education (1995–2004).

The World Court and the ICC

When Americans think of the rule of law, one of the first images that springs to mind is the courtroom scene, dominated by the imposing figure of the robed judge, seated on high and flanked by the prosecutor, the defendant, and the jury box, with a silent, respectful audience sitting in front. Although the UN is not a government, it does have courts and tribunals, some of them as imposing and solemn as any in the United States. Most of them focus on human rights, with one exception, and two of them figure often in the news media and therefore are probably known to most people, at least by name.

The International Court of Justice, also known as the World Court, is one of the six principal organs of the UN. Based in The Hague, it is the sole UN court that can hear all kinds of cases, involving not just human rights but any legal issue over which governments may differ with each other. The court hears only those cases involving states, not individuals, based on the voluntary participation of the governments concerned. Once a national government agrees to have its case heard at the court, it must comply with the ensuing judgment. The court also gives advisory opinions on legal questions at the request of international organizations. Its fifteen judges, each serving nine-year terms, are elected through a complicated procedure by the Security Council and the General Assembly. No two judges may be nationals of the same state. The World Court's first case was about a boundary jurisdiction involving the United Kingdom and Albania and was filed in May 1947.

The other court, the International Criminal Court (ICC), is solely a criminal tribunal, and it is a newcomer to the global community. Strictly speaking, it is an independent body, and its prosecutors and eighteen judges are not formally part of the UN. They are accountable only to the countries that have ratified the Rome Statute (1998), which established the court.

The UN helped found the ICC to address a problem that, in a sense, the UN helped create. Through conventions, treaties, and other documents, the UN has constructed a framework for civilized behavior in most aspects of life, even war. Unfortunately, in recent decades a new wave of crimes has appeared, as combatants and innocent bystanders find themselves engaged in civil wars and other forms of internal conflict involving guerrillas, paramilitary groups, or terrorists. Atrocities and even genocide can result when the restraints of military training and moral limitations are forgotten.

Until recently there were no international courts for trying persons accused of committing atrocities, except for special tribunals such as the one at Nuremberg after World War II. The Security Council tried to fill this gap through the creation of special tribunals designed to bring justice to nations ravaged by civil war. The council created the first such tribunal in 1993 to deal with massacres in the former Yugoslavia. Staffed by 1,200 employees and operating out of The Hague, the tribunal has taken into custody and is trying persons indicted for war crimes. In 1994 the Security Council established another tribunal to examine the genocide in Rwanda; it has a staff of approximately 900 and is based in Kigali, Rwanda. In 2000, a special court was set up in Sierra Leone to try those accused of committing atrocities against civilians and attacking UN forces disarming and demobilizing the combatants after a civil war. The United States applauded the formation of the UN tribunals and has been their most generous donor. In 2000, for example, its assessed and voluntary contributions amounted to about $53 million.

The ICC institutionalizes the concept of the international tribunal for crimes against humanity. However, the court is not a venue of first resort. Instead, individuals accused of committing a crime against humanity must be tried by their government if it has ratified the treaty. The accused would come before the ICC only if their home country was unable or unwilling to act. In order to prevent malicious or frivolous accusations, the statute requires prosecutors to justify their decisions according to generally recognized principles that would exclude politically motivated charges.

When the Rome Treaty came to the United States for ratification, it got a cool reception. The Clinton administration signed it with reservations based on concerns about the possibility of capricious prosecutions. The George W. Bush administration stated that it would not send the treaty to Congress for ratification without major changes aimed at protecting US military and government personnel against "politically motivated war crimes prosecutions." The Bush administration also removed the US signature from the treaty, to the satisfaction of many in Congress, who claimed it violated US sovereignty.

Even though the White House and Congress resisted ratification, the rest of the world made the ICC a reality. The Rome Treaty gained

> **Security Council Special Tribunals**
>
> International Criminal Tribunal for the Former Yugoslavia (1993)
> International Criminal Tribunal for Rwanda (1994)
> Special Court for Sierra Leone (2002)
> Special Tribunal for Lebanon (2007)

enough signatures to establish the court, and it was officially inaugurated at The Hague in 2003. The ICC began trying its first case in 2007, with the filing of charges against an alleged militia leader from the Democratic Republic of the Congo for "enlisting, conscripting and using children under the age of fifteen to participate actively in hostilities." In 2008, the court's prosecutor, Luis Moreno-Ocampo of Argentina, was investigating three other situations in the Central African Republic, northern Uganda, and the Darfur region of Sudan and also asked the judges to issue a precedent-setting arrest warrant for Sudan's president, Hassan al-Bashir, for complicity in war crimes in Darfur.

There are signs that the US government may be softening its stance against the ICC, opening the possibility that the tribunal might someday be approved by the entire world community. In a speech at The Hague in June 2007, the State Department's legal adviser, John B. Bellinger III, reminded his listeners that in 1990 Congress had actually called for the creation of an international crime tribunal very much like the ICC, but only if it met certain criteria, including "respect for national sovereignty." The ICC did not meet these criteria, Bellinger declared, and that is why the US government had not become a party to it.

Bellinger went to assure his listeners, however, that the United States shared a commitment to "ensuring accountability for genocide, war crimes, and crimes against humanity." The United States did not object when the Security Council referred alleged crimes in wartorn Darfur to the ICC, Bellinger noted, and it stated a willingness to assist the ICC prosecutor's Darfur investigation, "should we receive an appropriate request." These various acts, said Bellinger, "reflect our desire to find practical ways to work with ICC supporters to advance our shared goals of promoting international criminal justice." Perhaps the most conciliatory statement came at the end of his discussion of the ICC, when he said, "It is in our common interest to find a modus vivendi on the ICC based on mutual respect for the positions of both sides."

A Council, not a Commission

Most legal and rights issues do not require a trial in the courtroom, of course. Courts are expensive instruments, and trying cases can consume great amounts of time and money. Therefore, both in the United States and the UN, it is usually faster and more efficient to operate through negotiation and discussion, with the aim of finding a mutually acceptable solution that will also be legally and morally sound. In the UN, the main venue for examining human rights issues and resolving problems was given to the Commission on Human Rights, created in 1946, and chaired originally by none other than Eleanor Roosevelt. For decades the commission was the main UN body for making human rights policy and providing a forum for discussion. It met each year in Geneva, Switzerland, and held public meetings on violations of human rights. When necessary, it appointed experts, called special rapporteurs, to examine rights abuses or conditions in specific countries.

Unfortunately, the commission soon gained a reputation for biases against certain nations, such as Israel and the United States, while turning a blind eye to gross rights abuses by authoritarian regimes such as those in China, Russia, and Iran. Observers commented ironically that the commission's members often included nations notorious for their failure to observe the human rights standards that the commission was supposed to be monitoring.

The behavior of the commission became such a scandal among US and European observers and media that something drastic had to be done. The General Assembly finally agreed to abolish the commission and replace it with a new body called the Human Rights Council,

The Human Rights Council meets in Geneva, March 28, 2007. UN Photo/ Mark Garten

organized to fix the problems of its predecessor. Or at least that was the intention.

The forty-seven-member council was inaugurated in June 2006, but it soon began drawing as much criticism as its predecessor, and from the same critics. "Our original idea, which the Europeans shared," says former US ambassador John Bolton, "was that we would have a whole series of procedural changes to the new Human Rights Council that in the aggregate would result in a different kind of membership in the Human Rights Commission, so that you wouldn't have those abusers of human rights or simply countries that didn't much care about human rights and were on the commission just because it was a good thing to be on." The members of the new council, however, included China, Russia, and Saudi Arabia, whose human rights records were called "dismal" by one press account.

John Bolton accuses the Europeans of failing to push for reforms that the United States wanted, "so that the new body was not going to be that much different from the prior body, and in fact that's exactly what happened. That's one reason we voted against it in 2006, because we said it's not much different from the Human Rights Commission." Rights expert Ruth Wedgwood agrees that the Europeans did not push hard enough for meaningful changes in the new council. "The attempted reform was done too quickly," she argues. "The number of countries was only slightly cut down and the predominance of the South was increased. With regional loyalties, even on human rights issues, this made it more likely that the council would spend the bulk of its disposable time on Israel and Palestine." UN insider Jeffrey Laurenti is similarly critical of "this crazy drive to shrink it," which meant the loss of four Western seats. "What were these people thinking?" he asks.

The new council's track record seems to bear out these largely pessimistic assessments. The council's members include states with poor human rights records, and its deliberations so far have been dominated by condemnations of Israel. In 2007–8, the council passed eighteen country-specific resolutions, nine of them censures of Israel.

From the other side of the aisle, however, the council doesn't look so flawed. According to Pakistan's former ambassador Akram, the old Human Rights Commission was accused of being "a one-sided body, a politicized body and ineffective in defending human rights," and therefore it was proposed to create a smaller council "to keep the riffraff out so that the major powers could have a smaller body in which they could take the 'right' decisions." According to Akram, the developing countries argued that whatever the size of the proposed council, "it should reflect the actual composition of the General Assembly and the regional groups in the General Assembly." Since, by his math, more than 130 of the 192 UN member nations fall into the developing category, they should arguably constitute the great majority of members of the Human Rights Council.

That is actually how the council was set up, remarks Akram, and "some of our friends in the North are not happy about that." It was mere coincidence, he continues, that when the council began its work, unrest and war broke out in Lebanon and Gaza, so of course the council addressed those events. The Europeans had insisted that a special session of the council could be called by only one-third of the members. "Well, guess what: two can play the game," says Akram, "and therefore special sessions were called by our Arab friends on Palestine and Lebanon, and now it's been said that the council is targeting Israel. But conditions and procedures were dictated by the very same countries that are complaining about it right now."

Ruth Wedgwood sees the council's actions as evidence that the old politics may be rearing its head again. She is especially concerned that North–South issues may tarnish one of the procedural safeguards that the Europeans managed to retain in the new council, the universal periodic review. That is a regular process of issuing reports on the compliance of each UN member nation with human rights norms, including its obligations under the specific human rights treaties that it has joined. Of course, such reports are meaningful only if conducted in an impartial and rigorous manner, and they could be positively dangerous if countries lie about their handling of rights. "The great fear now," she says, "is that the Universal Periodic Review process, rather than discouraging attempts to dominate the council on the part of illiberal and even brutal regimes, will instead end up undermining the authority of the treaty bodies to insist upon observance of each of the covenants."

Hillel Neuer, who directs UN Watch, a human rights NGO based in Geneva, thinks the undermining is already happening. "Regrettably," he says, "the thirty-two reviews so far have been toothless, with most states praising each other or limiting their challenges to softball questions." Yet he does not think the United States can afford to ignore the council. "The United States should join," he argues, "because the HRC, however disappointing, is a permanent forum of international influence."

Meanwhile, the General Assembly, through its Third Committee, has regained some importance as an alternative venue for advancing the cause of human rights. "Only there can one still pass a resolution against abuses by Iran, Belarus, and other major violators," says

Neuer. "Violators now dominate the smaller council, and the universal body of the GA has become, relative to the HRC, a more favorable body for addressing pressing violations." He concedes that the window of opportunity is small, however, because the Third Committee meets only a few months of each year.

For Wedgwood, the concern is not the UN's ability to frame human rights issues: "On simply framing normative statements, the UN often does very good work." She praises the human rights treaties as being "a great step forward" for many countries. "Are UN experts sometimes unrealistic on the difficulties of governance?" Yes, she says, but the successes are beyond dispute. "To advance the purposes of the Human Rights Council, we should try to protect it from the biases of regional politics." Fixing the Human Rights Council is likely to be a hot topic in 2011, when the council is reviewed by the General Assembly.

The High Commissioner

Criticisms of the new council sometimes obscure the presence of another force in the UN rights establishment. In 1993, the General Assembly established the post of UN high commissioner for human rights, responsible to the secretary-general. The high commissioner is charged with being a secretariat for the Human Rights Council, overseeing the UN's human rights activities, helping develop rights standards, and promoting international cooperation to expand and protect rights. The office does not control the Human Rights Council, nor does it have much influence over it or its special rapporteurs. Perhaps for that reason, the US government has cultivated good relations with the high commissioner and sought to "build a strong cooperative relationship," in the words of a recent State Department report.

"The high commissioner's role is not defined, so it's up to each high commissioner," says Wedgwood. "There have been only four high commissioners so far," she adds. "Part of the work of the overall job is to help coordinate the development of the jurisprudence of the now numerous treaty bodies. This has been a challenge because each of the committees is made up of volunteers and has its own trajectory. You also have the problem of countries having to report on multiple topics to multiple treaty bodies and of the committees potentially taking different views of issues." The first high commissioner was José Ayala-Lasso of Ecuador, who was succeeded in 1997 by Mary Robinson, former president of Ireland. Her successor was Louise Arbour of Canada. In 2008 Ban Ki-moon named South African judge Navenethem (Navi) Pillay as the next commissioner. She is the former president of the International Criminal Tribunal for Rwanda and holds a degree from Harvard University.

The Responsibility to Protect (R2P)

Everyone is "for" human rights, of course, but people may not agree on how to define or enforce rights when they seem to conflict with national boundaries. If mass murder is committed within a nation— something that has happened with lamentable frequency lately—does the world community have the obligation or the right to intervene to stop it? The usual response over the decades has been no. And yet, the spirit of the UN Charter clearly should lead member states to act when human rights are being grossly violated.

Kofi Annan proposed to alter the historical approach radically by arguing that international human rights law must apply in each member state and that certain acts, such as genocide, cannot be allowed to occur with impunity. He based his view, no doubt, on his own bitter experience with events in places like Bosnia and Rwanda, where the UN was accused of doing too little to prevent mass murders.

Annan formally stated his new approach to intervention in an address at the General Assembly in September 1999, in which he asked member states "to unite in the pursuit of more effective policies to stop organized mass murder and egregious violations of human rights." Conceding that there were many ways to intervene, he asserted that not only diplomacy but even armed action was an acceptable option. This provoked debate around the world. Rights organizations generally supported Annan's comments. The international human rights NGO

Human Rights Watch hailed his statement as a "highlight" of 1999, a year when "sovereignty gave way in places where crimes against humanity were being committed." Others were less happy. They feared that the concept of "humanitarian intervention" might disguise unjustified interference in a nation's affairs or might encourage secessionist movements to provoke gross violations of human rights in order to bring on an international presence that might aid their cause.

Acknowledging the value of arguments put forth by critics and skeptics, Annan posed a difficult question: "If humanitarian intervention is, indeed, an unacceptable assault on sovereignty, how should we respond to a Rwanda, to a Srebrenica—to gross and systematic violations of human rights that offend every precept of our common humanity?" He laid out the issues very clearly: "But surely no legal principle—not even sovereignty—can ever shield crimes against humanity. Where such crimes occur and peaceful attempts to halt them have been exhausted, the Security Council has a moral duty to act on behalf of the international community. The fact that we cannot protect people everywhere is no reason for doing nothing when we can. Armed intervention must always remain the option of last resort, but in the face of mass murder it is an option that cannot be relinquished."

At Annan's urging, the world's leaders, assembled at a UN summit in September 2005, voted to adopt his concept under the term "responsibility to protect," often abbreviated as R2P. The concept actually derives from ideas first stated by Australian diplomat Gareth Evans and then elaborated by the International Commission on Intervention and State Sovereignty, established by the Canadian government in 2000.

Edward Luck, an expert on R2P, praises Annan for "putting humanitarian intervention on the map and the dilemma facing the international community." He also recognizes that R2P has become an extremely controversial issue. Ruth Wedgwood criticizes the concept for lacking any means of enforcement. "The R2P is a paper tiger at the moment. . . . People don't realize that it is a humanitarian-military commitment, not just a political commitment." She is making the obvious point that humanitarian intervention may require the application of military force, yet some of the staunchest supporters of R2P are actually reducing their armed forces. "Europe is visibly demilitarizing, and therefore you are left with a vacuum. If you will not invest in the capacity to put people in the field with arms, then it's just a right to protect by rhetoric." She sees a "complete mismatch" between European ethical aspirations "and their willingness to use defensive force."

Pakistan's former permanent representative Akram, like some other observers, has a different criticism. He sees R2P as merely "a slogan," and not even a necessary one. "International humanitarian law already allows the international community to act in cases where there are such crimes—war crimes, genocide, crimes against humanity," he maintains. "You don't need new decisions or new conventions for that purposes."

He continues, "Wherever there has been genocide—in Srebrenica or Rwanda—in recent years, it has been because of the failure of the great powers to allow the international community to act. Srebrenica, we know what happened: the Security Council would not send troops to protect those defenseless people, who we knew were going to be slaughtered, and the Dutch troops stood by while the slaughter happened. So where is the R2P?" Akram concludes that responsibility for failing to protect lies not with the developing countries but with the major powers: "And therefore this is an exercise to salve their conscience."

It is not yet clear whether R2P will prevail or expire in neglect. Ban Ki-moon has demonstrated his willingness to tackle difficult issues, even those where he may differ from the position of many developing nations and powerful member states like Russia. Stating his support for R2P, he has appointed a full-time senior adviser on genocide and other atrocities and in February 2008 named Edward Luck as special adviser on R2P. Madeleine Albright thinks Ban is doing the right thing. "The secretary-general keeps pushing," she says, "and ultimately we have to show that the concept of national sovereignty and the responsibility to protect can work together."

CHAPTER 13

UN Finances

I'd like to have a Ferrari, but since I can't afford it, I'm probably going to get a cheaper car when I leave this job. So therefore, we have to work hard with the Secretariat, with the other member states, to do what we must, what we can afford, but the whole budget process needs to be looked at to make it more rational, to make the presentation a single budget comprehensively so the members can make a determination.

—Zalmay Khalilzad, former US ambassador to the UN

There is no free lunch, not even at the United Nations. Each month the UN's financial office sends out millions of dollars' worth of checks to pay for staff salaries, computer services, electricity, technical consultants, housekeeping for its big New York City headquarters, and a thousand other things. When you add all these costs, from all the members of the UN family, including the various agencies and committees, the total runs into many billions each year. Where does the money come from? Not from taxes. The UN is not a government, so it cannot levy taxes. The bulk of the dollars comes from the UN members themselves.

Think of the UN as a condo apartment house, we'll call it Global

> ## Money Talks
>
> "The test of the American commitment to the UN, above all, is financial. That's what tests it, and whether we seek to strengthen the UN through a combination of resources and reform or weaken it through neglect and punishment."
> —Richard Holbrooke, former US ambassador to the UN

Towers, located on prime real estate on the east side of Manhattan in New York City, with a breathtaking view of the cityscape and the East River. Periodically the condo owner-members (nation-states) meet to vote on setting a budget for the coming years, based on regular membership fees, voluntary contributions, and occasional special assessments. Discussion invariably focuses on how big the expense budget should be and how the costs should be allocated among the owners, who vary widely in wealth, outlook, and commitment to keeping the condo safe, comfortable, and solvent.

As in any condo where the owners are well known to one another, the budget debate inevitably runs along ruts worn through decades of meetings, with occasional sharp exchanges when divergent opinions clash. Something of this sort unfolds in the General Assembly's Fifth Committee (Budgetary and Administrative) every three years as it deliberates on the scale and nature of the general UN budget. That is when the General Assembly can really flex its muscles, because its budget decisions affect all parts of Global Towers, from the airy thirty-eighth-floor office of the secretary-general to the stuffy basement where the building engineers make their daily rounds. It is estimated that the annual operating budgets of the Secretariat, other UN organs, peacekeeping, and the UN agencies, funds, and programs, excluding the World Bank and the International Monetary Fund, come to some $20 billion each year.

The Budget Process

Membership in the UN comes with the obligation to help pay for its support—something that has never been questioned. Instead, the focus has been on the size of each member state's contribution. Financial support takes three basic forms. First is the mandatory assessment for the general UN budget, also referred to as the "regular" or "administrative" budget, which funds the Secretariat and related bodies. Second is the mandatory assessment for the peacekeeping budget, which as the name suggests funds the peacekeeping missions and related UN bodies. And third are voluntary contributions that member states make for specific UN programs and groups or organizations, such as the United Nations Children's Fund (UNICEF) or the World Food Program (WFP). Finally, there are occasional special assessments, like the $1.9 billion that the members are scheduled to pay to renovate the New York City headquarters.

Most discussions in the media relate to the "regular budget," which pays for activities, staff, and basic infrastructure but not peacekeeping. In 2008, this was approximately $2.6 billion. (The regular budget is for a two-year period, a biennium, so $2.6 billion is simply half of the $5.2 billion that the General Assembly approved when it voted on the budget.) The formulas for calculating a nation's assessed contributions for the regular budget and the peacekeeping budget are based largely on the country's share of the world economy. In other words, the rich pay more than the poor. Nations with a low per-capita income get a discount, as do those with a high level of foreign debt. The United States, having the world's largest economy by a wide margin, naturally pays the largest share, about 22 percent, and very poor nations pay a nominal amount. The poorest nations have to pay a minimum of about $19,248 annually for their UN dues.

The regular budget is the product of a complicated process designed to ensure that all interested parties have their say in how funds are obtained and spent. The secretary-general proposes a draft budget and gives it to the Advisory Committee on Administrative and Budgetary Questions (ACABQ) for review. The advisory committee consists

Why Renovate?

The UN recently began a $1.9 billion renovation of its landmark headquarters building in New York City. Why? Experts agree that the building, which has had little but ordinary maintenance since it was completed in 1951, needs major updating, both to meet twenty-first-century needs and to bring it into conformance with local fire and safety codes. According to a letter to the UN written by Marjorie B. Tiven, the city's UN commissioner, inspectors cited the building for 866 safety violations in 2006 and 2007, and in 2008, the New York Fire Department advised the UN to cancel all tours of the building, which draw half a million people annually. When the UN decided to continue the tours, the city's school system declared that it would not allow teachers to bring their students to the building.

UN Budget 2008

Regular: $2.6 billion
Peacekeeping: $6.8 billion (July 2007–June 2008)

of sixteen individuals nominated by their governments, usually including a US national, and elected by the General Assembly. The Committee for Programme and Coordination (CPC), consisting of thirty-four experts elected by the General Assembly, reviews the program aspects of the budget. Unlike the advisory committee, in which the experts serve in their personal capacity, the program committee experts represent the views of their governments. The revised draft is sent to the General Assembly's Fifth Committee for approval. The committee makes a final adjustment and then votes to approve the budget, which it then sends to the General Assembly for a vote by the full membership of the UN. That vote makes the document the official UN general budget for the next biennium. Each country has the opportunity to suggest changes in the draft budget, but the changes may not necessarily be adopted.

Peacekeeping is treated separately from other budgets. The scale used to make peacekeeping assessments has ten levels of support, with the least-developed countries paying 10 percent of what they would have owed according to the assessment scale for the regular budget and the five permanent Security Council members paying a surcharge of about 25 percent. In 2001, the US share of peacekeeping costs was reduced from 31 percent to about 27 percent.

The UN's agencies, commissions, and programs have their own budgets. Each director draws up a budget and sends it to the secretary-general, who incorporates the information into the overall UN budget, which is sent to the General Assembly's Fifth Committee. Most agencies, commissions, and programs also raise funds independently from member states and other sources. When Mark Malloch Brown was head of the United Nations Development Programme, he answered a query about his organization's budget this way: "I call it $1.2 billion, and there are two other numbers which others use. One is $750 million, which is core contributions. I call it $1.2 billion because that's core plus donor contributions to special trust funds for special issues. Some call it $2 billion because that includes what we call co-financing, where developed countries kick in a huge volume of resources because they like us, in many cases, to spend their money for them. I count that out because for various reasons not dealt with it's a little misleading. So I say $1.2 billion, pessimists say $750 million, the optimists say $2 billion or $2.1. And it's growing. Last year the core in dollar terms grew 4 percent." Is that perfectly clear?

Sharing a Growing Burden

One of the most surprising fiscal events at the UN has been the large and rapid escalation of budgets since about 2002. For example, annual peacekeeping costs peaked at $3.5 billion in 1994, during the large-scale operations in the former Yugoslavia, dropped to $1.3 bil-

lion in 1997, and rose toward the $3 billion level in 2002. After that
they began climbing steeply as the United States and other Security
Council members began authorizing the creation of more peacekeeping missions. The budget for 2008 was $7 billion, the highest ever.
The general, or regular, budget has experienced a similar increase,
from $2.5 billion for the 2000–2001 biennium, to $3.6 billion in
2004–5, $4.1 billion in 2006–7, and $5.2 billion in 2008–9.

The increase occurred during the Bush administration and is at-
tributed by some observers in part to US requests for a greater UN
presence around the world, especially in countries of interest to the
United States. Fiscal conservatives in the United States are understandably alarmed at this development. Former US ambassador John
Bolton calls it "a breakdown of a twenty-year-long effort to rein in UN
spending."

Even these escalating budget figures are pretty small potatoes in
today's world of trillion-dollar economies. For example, the UN's web
site once noted that "the budget for UN worldwide human rights
activities is smaller than that of the Zürich Opera House." That may
be true, but not every member state can afford the cost of the Zürich
Opera House, and so questions often arise about how to allocate fiscal
obligations to avoid overburdening very small or poor nations. Most
discussions about excessive burdens have actually focused not on the
poorest nations, however, but on some of the richest. The United
States and Japan have been the largest contributors to the UN budgets, and both have asked for downward adjustments in what they pay.
The United States and Japan together paid nearly 41.5 percent of the
2006 general budget. In FY 2006, the United States contributed
some $5.3 billion to the UN family, including $870 million to peacekeeping. The United States is also typically the major donor for certain
agencies and programs, such the World Food Programme (41.5 percent of the 2006 budget) and the UN High Commissioner for Refugees (24 percent), to name just two.

The United States has negotiated several reductions in its share of
the general budget. For example, in 1974 the UN agreed to place a cap

of 25 percent on the size of a member state's assessment, effectively lowering the United States' share in subsequent years. Another change came in 2000, when the General Assembly reduced the US share of the regular budget to a maximum of 22 percent, and its share of peacekeeping costs from 31 percent to about 27 percent. Both reductions came at the urging of the US government, in response to the Helms-Biden Law, which stipulated that the United States would pay nearly $1 billion in assessment arrears over three years if the UN met certain conditions, such as a reduction in the assessment rate.

The Japanese government took a different approach to trying to reduce its assessment. In 2006, it proposed that the UN put a floor of 3 or 5 percent under the regular-budget contributions of the P5. In other words, a permanent member of the Security Council would have to pay an annual assessment of at least 3 or 5 percent of the total general budget. When the Japanese made this proposal, China was paying only 2 percent and Russia 1 percent of the general budget, compared with 19 percent for Japan and 22 percent for the U.S. Raising the Chinese and Russian assessment would permit reductions in those of other nations, including Japan's.

Despite adjustments, the United States and several other large developed nations remain major funders of the UN (table 4). The ten largest contributors provide nearly three-quarters of the regular budget. The influential Group of 77, by contrast, typically pay less than 10 percent of the general budget yet represent 130 member states, or more than two-thirds of UN members.

The G-77 and other blocs in the General Assembly have voting power far beyond what one would expect based on their financial contributions to the UN, and the discrepancy has led to friction in the assembly. As a concession to some of the wealthier and more highly assessed members states, in 1988 the assembly and its Fifth Committee began passing UN budgets by consensus. This was intended to give the wealthier states some leverage in the budget process.

The consensus approach ruled until very recently, when the United States and about fifty other nations voted against a budget resolution

Table 4. Ten most highly assessed members for regular budget, 2008

Member state	Share of general budget (percent)
United States	22
Japan	19
Germany	9
United Kingdom	6
France	6
Italy	5
Canada	3
Spain	3
China	2
Mexico	2
Subtotal	76
All 182 other members	24
Grand total	100

Source: Adapted from UN web site, "Image and Reality about the UN," chapter 5.

Note: Numbers may not total 100 percent due to rounding.

in 2006. The United States again insisted on a taking a vote for another budget resolution, the one for 2008–9, because it objected to the "piecemeal" process by which it was being assembled.

Complaints about process and equitable sharing of burdens have led some insiders, such as former ambassador Bolton, to propose that the leading nations lobby for a fundamental revision in the nature of UN funding. "What we really need is not additional effort for marginal change but a major change in the way the whole UN is funded, to move toward voluntary contributions. That's the only way to get people interested [in UN reform]." He accepts the need for the United States to take the lead but is sure that other donors such as Japan will welcome it. "They will fall in behind us," he says, "but as usual at the UN we would have to be the ones who really press it."

The Arrears

Ideally, each member state accepts its assessment as being appropriate and immediately sends a check to the UN for the full amount. Reality is more complicated. Even for routine and predictable budgets, like the regular budget, the UN has a hard time getting everyone to pay fully and on time. By May 31, 2002, for example, only eighty members, some 40 percent of the membership, had paid their annual dues, leaving the UN waiting for 110 countries. Some member-states delay their payments for various reasons, usually unrelated to their ability to pay, while others (like the United States) pay on their own schedule, depending on when their legislature or national assembly votes the funds.

The Charter (Article 19) permits the UN to penalize a member that is two years in arrears by taking away its vote in the General Assembly. This has been done quite a bit, as a last resort. The United States has found itself in danger of penalization during years when it was withholding its dues or paying them slowly to express its unhappiness with the UN. In fact, of all member states the United States typically has the largest payments arrears to the general and peacekeeping budgets. For 2006, the United States accounted for $1 billion, or 43 percent, of the amount owed by member states, and for 2007, the nation accounted for about half of all arrears for the combined regular and peacekeeping budgets. Congress primarily bears the responsibility for this consistent pattern because its process of appropriating funds lags behind the UN funding calendar. And if, in addition, Congress is late agreeing on a federal budget, as happened in fiscal year 2007, it may appropriate only a partial payment of the UN dues and postpone full payment until a final budget has been approved.

The arrears problem, like the debate over assessments, has generated many suggestions about a variety of possible fixes, including even a global tax on currency transactions, but they haven't gone beyond talk. As the authors of one recent study comment, "Member states responsible for the highest contributions are reluctant to reform the system, fearing they would lose political leverage." One UN insider, Shepard Forman, has offered his own solution. "I once suggested

From the UN Charter, Chapter IV

ARTICLE 19

A Member of the United Nations which is in arrears in the payment of its financial contributions to the Organization shall have no vote in the General Assembly if the amount of its arrears equals or exceeds the amount of the contributions due from it for the preceding two full years. The General Assembly may, nevertheless, permit such a Member to vote if it is satisfied that the failure to pay is due to conditions beyond the control of the Member.

rather facetiously," he says, "that there should be a reverse scale of assessments in which countries that act badly and therefore cost the UN more ... should have to pay more dues. There should be a system where if you misbehave very badly your membership should be suspended or something else occurs." By that rationale, Iraq's former dictator Saddam Hussein should have been one of the UN's greatest benefactors.

Nations in Arrears

In May 2008, seven member states were in arrears under the terms of Article 19:
Central African Republic
Comoros
Guinea-Bissau
Liberia
São Tomé and Príncipe
Somalia
Tajikistan
The General Assembly, citing extenuating circumstances, permitted these countries to exercise their vote until the end of its sixty-second session.

CHAPTER 14

The Call for Reform

The world is changing around us, and the U.N. must change with it. We are responsible to the world's taxpayers . . . to create an organization that is more effective and more modern.

—Ban Ki-moon, secretary-general of the United Nations

In the opening months of 2004, reports began to appear in the press suggesting that the UN's largest humanitarian program was being used by Iraq's Saddam Hussein regime to generate billions of dollars in illegal kickbacks. The Oil-for-Food Programme was part of the aftermath of the first Gulf War, fought in 1991, when an international coalition of forces acting under the authority of the Security Council threw Iraqi invaders out of Kuwait. The Security Council imposed sweeping sanctions when Iraq invaded Kuwait, but soon the sanctions were perceived as hurting not only the Saddam Hussein regime but also innocent Iraqis.

The Security Council created the Oil-for-Food Programme to fix that problem. Oil-for-Food was intended to provide a way for the Iraqi government, under UN supervision, to sell crude oil for buying food and other civilian necessities but not arms. During its existence (until

2003) the program generated $67 billion in oil revenue and $31 billion in humanitarian assistance, according to a US government report published in 2006. The program met its humanitarian goals, the report states, thus "averting a humanitarian crisis while limiting Iraq's ability to purchase military-related items." But "internal control problems allowed the . . . Iraqi regime to manipulate the program and circumvent sanctions to obtain billions of dollars in illicit payments."

Based on the initial press reports, observers quickly smelled a scandal. Estimates of just how much money Saddam Hussein extorted through the program varied from about $7.5 billion to as much as $21 billion, much of it the fault of the UN, according to some critics. Friends of the UN were upset that the world body might have inadvertently helped support a despot, while detractors of the UN began issuing I-told-you-so statements about bureaucratic corruption, lax oversight, favoritism, and pervasive ineptitude.

As the scandal unfolded, even Kofi Annan's son became a factor owing to his business contacts with one of the participating commercial enterprises that was dealing with the Baghdad regime. Rarely has the UN gotten such a black eye in public as it did with Oil-for-Food.

The Need for Reforms

The Oil-for-Food scandal put new force into efforts by many countries, experts, and other stakeholders to "reform" the UN. The controversy we reviewed in chapter 5 about reforming the Security Council to make it more reflective of modern times has a parallel in the administrative side of the UN. For decades, voices from many corners have been calling for reforms, or at least improvements, in most of the bodies, agencies, and activities of the UN family. The calls are fed in part by concern that the UN system could be much more effective, efficient, and accountable than it is and in part by allegations that the bureaucracy has been a juicy career plum for a small group of staff who put their interests ahead of those of the organization.

The most outspoken proponents of reform have usually come from the large donor nations, and many of them are actually quite friendly

Leading the Way

Working cooperatively with the international community and engaging in multilateral organizations can be an important and cost-effective means for furthering national security interests of the United States. The United Nations provides a forum for the US to build support for global action on enduring foreign policy interests, such as international stability, prosperity, and the promotion of fundamental freedoms. Through burden sharing, the UN allows us to advance our goals without paying all the bills or taking all the risks.
—Hillary Rodham Clinton, US secretary of state

to the UN, which they want to make better. Former US ambassador Richard Holbrooke argues that the UN "is the flawed but indispensable institution that we have two choices with: weaken it by undermining it or trying to strengthen it by getting it to correct its flaws." For him, the choice is obvious: "In America when we discern flaws we try to fix them. We should do the same with the UN because in the end, it's a highly leveraged organization that helps America and the nation's interest and world. But what a mess it is."

The UN's Response

One of the first substantive efforts by the UN to address the criticisms came in 1994 with the establishment of the Office of Internal Oversight Services, charged with making the bureaucracy more effective and efficient. Creation of the office pleased the US government, which described it as "one of the most significant management reforms adopted by the General Assembly in many years."

When Kofi Annan took office in 1997, he launched what he called his "quiet revolution," to streamline the organization and make it both more efficient and more effective without raising costs. The quiet revolution managed to stop the Secretariat's budget creep for a few years, beginning in 1998, and even reduced it a little. Although the UN claimed that the total number of all staff in the UN system (about

52,000) was much smaller than the number of employees at many large corporations, it nevertheless tried to keep staff numbers from growing too fast. The Secretariat's staff fell from about 12,000 in 1984–85 to 8,900. The Secretariat gained a new reform tool in December 2000, when the General Assembly authorized it to start "results-based budgeting." Long urged by the United States as a way of rationalizing the allocation and spending of funds, results-based budgeting establishes objectives for each department or program and develops "performance indicators" to measure progress in reaching them.

Most observers credit Annan's quiet revolution with making real improvements. Former US ambassador Nancy Soderberg thinks that Kofi Annan tossed out a lot of the deadwood. "I would say that 90 percent are terrific. You have the young people who are very enthused about it and the senior people who have worked their life in the UN and loved it, and then you have a few people scattered around who are there for life."

One of the most objective and carefully reasoned analyses of UN administrative reform came in May 2000, from the US government's General Accounting Office. The report was generally positive, much to everyone's surprise. It praised the restructuring of the UN's leadership and operations but warned that the main reform objectives had not yet been achieved, particularly the goal of holding the Secretariat accountable for "accomplishing missions" rather than merely "carrying out activities." The main barrier to change was the General Assembly, which insisted on passing excessive numbers of resolutions for the Secretariat to carry out. In the most recent two-year period, the GA had more than doubled the number of its resolutions, and fully one-fifth of them "had vague or open-ended expectations." The report further noted that while coordination among agencies in the field had improved, much remained to be done in that regard. Richard Holbrooke is blunter: "The field coordination is appalling, and the agencies in the field have no real single head. They have a coordinator system that doesn't work."

Mark Malloch Brown makes a somewhat different criticism of the bureaucracy, citing a pervasive "disconnect between merit and re-

Paul Volcker briefs the General Assembly on the Oil-for-Food report, October 27, 2005. UN Photo/Mark Garten

ward." He notes, "There's something rational that if you work hard and do well, you get promoted, and if you don't work hard you don't. In parts of the UN that doesn't happen." He advocates "reconnect[ing] merit to make the UN again an international meritocracy." To do this, however, Malloch Brown believes that the UN must stop promoting on the basis of political correctness that encourages promoting staff proportionately from certain regions of the world. Asia, Africa, and other so-called less developed regions now offer a large pool of talented, skilled, and highly motivated professionals, he argues, that the UN ought to make more use of. These individuals are so highly qualified, he believes, that they will readily move up through the UN system without need of the "cultural relativism which is used to promote incompetents."

A somewhat related point is often made by UN member states from the developing world, who complain that some of the most desirable senior posts within the Secretariat are filled under a "tradition" of

regional representation that favors the United States and other affluent nations. The point has been made forcefully by Ambassador
Munir Akram of Pakistan, who was recently head of the G-77. "The
major countries, the major powers hold very high positions in the
Secretariat and support their national interests and refuse to allow the
SG to cut departments," he claims. And when they do ask for budget
cuts, they do it "where it does not affect their national interests." He
labels this "a double standard which is applied or is thought to be
applied in the Secretariat, and we as overseers of the G-77 do not
accept this double standard."

Volcker Report: Oil-for-Food Programme

The Oil-for-Food scandal gave new point to reform efforts. Secretary
General Annan moved quickly to appoint an investigative body, the
Independent Inquiry Committee (IIC), chaired by Paul Volcker, a
highly respected former head of the Federal Reserve. His group's
findings, commonly referred to as the Volcker report, were released in
September 2005. They addressed the main allegations raised in the
scandal and listed steps that could be taken to prevent a recurrence.

Volcker's report generated a range of responses from experts and
officials. Some saw it as vindication of their past criticisms of the UN.
Former ambassador John Bolton says that "the most important thing
that can be concluded after examination of the whole scandal is when
Volcker said that the problems with Oil-for-Food were not unique, that
they reflected larger problems that were endemic within the UN itself."

Volcker himself has said that the Oil-for-Food Programme was not
well administered, but he also thought that it had achieved two of its
three main objectives. He offered his assessment in an interview with
William Luers, president of the United Nations Association of the
U.S.A., that was published in January 2008, more than two years after
the committee had issued its report. Alluding to the first goal, providing more food and nutrition to the Iraqi people, Volcker said it had
been achieved. And the program had been successful in the second
goal, to monitor and prevent any Iraqi efforts to acquire weapons of

mass destruction. The one deficiency was its inability to stop the sale of Iraqi oil that was not sanctioned by the program. The committee had strongly recommended important administrative reform, and Volcker thought there had been "some progress in implementation" during the previous two years.

Volcker put part of the blame for the scandal on the Security Council itself. He noted that the smuggling of oil by Iraq, which Oil-for-Food was supposed to curb, continued anyway, first through Jordan and later Turkey and Syria. And it was no secret. The United States government "justified not dealing with the smuggling in light of possible adverse effects on Jordan," one of its regional allies. The other P5 members also turned a blind eye to the smuggling, he declared. "The permanent members of the UN Security Council who were responsible for oversight did not raise objections or stop the smuggling." Volcker noted that "the Secretariat certainly should have brought these violations of the program to the attention of the UN Security Council," which "took little or no action on its own."

Volcker also explained in the interview (and his report) that most of the kickbacks were the result of deals made directly between Saddam Hussein's regime and approximately four thousand businesses, individuals, and national governments. "About two billion dollars was taken in connection with kickbacks related to Iraqi imports and from surcharges in the sale of oil," he noted, and went on to say that "about eight billion dollars flowed from the smuggling of oil outside the control of the Oil-For-Food-Program."

Volcker argued that "the Security Council itself, with its internal divisions and other priorities, in effect closed its eyes to evidence of smuggling or other illicit behavior. The UN Secretariat lacked internal controls and did not exercise adequate oversight of the program. The individuals in charge of administering the program and alerting the members of the UN Security Council came to know what was transpiring . . . but repeatedly failed to take action." Volcker also stated that "there is strong evidence that the senior UN official directly responsible for overseeing the program accepted some payment of about $165,000 with respect to the sale of some oil," an allegation that the official has denied.

UN Chief of Staff Mark Malloch Brown speaks at the Oil-for-Food probe press conference, 2005. UN Photo/Eskinder Debebe

Volcker then said that central to the failings of Oil-for-Food was "the failure of the UN to take its responsibility seriously at all levels of the organization. When internal controls and lines of responsibility are as weak as we found in our investigations and there is an absence of accountability, one has to assume that there was ample opportunity for corruption."

A complementary analysis of the scandal comes from New Zealand's former UN ambassador, Colin Keating, who is now director of Security Council Report, which issues a monthly analysis of the council's activities. "The Security Council was the biggest contributor" to the program's shortcomings, Keating claims, because "it actually created the atmosphere, the culture that the problems started to occur, married with the Secretariat's own culture. The two were a poisonous mix."

More Bells and Whistles

Of the two parts of the failure, the Secretariat began trying to fix one: its own administrative processes. The Procurement Task Force was established in January 2006, largely at the urging of then UN under-secretary-general for Management Christopher Burnham, with an annual budget of more than $10 million. It was charged with looking for corruption and abuse and providing information for prosecution. Burnham, a former official in the State Department, was appointed in May 2005 and left the UN in fall 2006. During his brief but energetic tenure he pushed for the creation of a UN Ethics Office, which officially opened in 2007. He is also credited with establishing a whistle-blower protection policy for UN staff; introducing international public sector accounting standards for the UN; and modernizing the UN's information and communication technology infrastructure.

Burnham's work overlapped with the tenure of Mark Malloch Brown as the deputy secretary-general. For him the main problem was managerial overload. "Oil-for-Food was a most extreme way of demonstrating the importance of a secretary-general being backed by a strong deputy to run the organization on his behalf," says Malloch Brown. The secretary-general, as the world's diplomat-in-chief, "does not have the time to apply the managerial rigor that this vast organization requires." Malloch Brown notes the importance of UN agencies and departments being able to cooperate smoothly with one another. "I saw very clearly how the system doesn't really want to allow that to happen," he complains. He found the General Assembly suspicious that the secretary-general was "ceding these kinds of management responsibilities to a Western deputy." And yet, "the powers were those which in any corporate setting would be seen as the powers not of a chief executive but of a chief operating officer." The division of responsibility was necessary and reasonable, says Malloch Brown, "unless you assume a secretary-general is to do everything, from turning off the lights at night to signing off on payroll every month."

Malloch Brown's experiences and the recommendations offered in the Volcker report suggest that even the most carefully and honestly administered UN staff must operate in a highly politicized environment, where others such as the Security Council and the General Assembly make the rules and can ignore them if they so choose. UN analyst Shepard Forman criticizes the UN precisely on this point: unlike the US government, he argues, "the UN doesn't have an effective system of checks and balances."

Reform is possible at the UN, as Burnham's efforts show, but it has certain limits, as Malloch Brown's experience demonstrates. From his vantage point as a highly placed advisor to the British government, Malloch Brown can take a broad view of the UN's situation. Progress on reform "is generally quite low," he thinks, despite the strong support of the new secretary-general. "My problem always is the demands on the UN grow exponentially, the rate of reform is a much lower trend line. It's a gentle uphill move whereas the demands on the UN rise vertically, so that the gap between expectation and performance continues to grow."

Perhaps the final word on the reform question should go to Richard Holbrooke, who cautions against harping excessively on the bureaucracy's failings. "We've got to be very careful as Americans not to be holier than thou because we have an inefficient bureaucracy as well, and ours is much larger and better funded."

CHAPTER 15

UN Agencies, Programs, and Commissions

More and more expectations are being placed on joining up UN responses on health, development, humanitarian aid: on WHO working with UNICEF, and UNFPA or the humanitarian agencies working together within a single recovery plan after a disaster. All these challenges . . . require cross-departmental, cross-agency, cross-funded management to make it happen.
—Mark Malloch Brown, former administrator of
the UN Development Programme

The Secretariat, Security Council, General Assembly, and other principal organs are the UN bodies that most command the public's attention. Yet they have only general oversight of the UN's huge array of global efforts to advance human rights, help refugees or earthquake victims, combat infectious diseases, and coordinate international trade, finance, development, and communications. The direct control of these vital activities is usually in the hands of entities known as programs, commissions, councils, and specialized agencies, which play key roles in the UN system. Some of the specialized agencies, for example, actually predate the UN, and many act quite independently.

These entities consist of nearly sixty organizations, divided into six

A Concise Definition of the UN

"The UN and its system of agencies represent the place where trans-national interests and constituencies seek to advance their agendas."
—Jeffrey Laurenti, Century Foundation

categories. Moving from left to right on the UN organizational chart (see the flowchart in chapter 1), we see first the "Programmes and Funds." Each of these was created to address an issue the General Assembly has deemed important. This is true also for the next category, "Other UN Entities," such as the Office of the High Commissioner for Human Rights, and for the Research and Training Institutes, such as the International Research and Training Institute for the Advancement of Women (INSTRAW). Moving to the upper right we have the commissions, of two types, "Functional" and "Regional." The remaining two boxes contain the "Related Organizations" and the "Specialized Agencies," which are autonomous organizations that have formal working relations with the UN. Their names show that the related organizations and specialized agencies cover virtually all areas of economic and social endeavor.

Coordination of these organizations is one of the greatest challenges facing the UN, for they have offices all over the map, with thousands of staff of all nationalities, and they address every imaginable issue. As a further complication, the categories of organizations each relate to the UN in a different way. The Administrative Committee on Coordination is charged with choreographing this far-flung ensemble.

To an outsider, these supporting organizations all look pretty much the same. Only the insider can perceive and fully appreciate their differences in terms of administrative position and prerogatives. The public, however, is more interested in the basics: what they do and how they do it. To find out what and how, a functional approach is best, because the organizations share many interests and methods of operation.

There are many ways of defining the major issues addressed by the agencies, programs, and commissions. Presented below are a set of selected issues: first comes human rights, followed by the related areas of economic and social development and the natural environment. Next comes disaster relief, then the control of dangerous agents like toxins and nuclear materials, and last the UN's role in globalization—first, in shaping world trade; second, in dealing with the expansion of international crime.

These categories are hardly definitive, but they do enable us to look at the supporting organizations in a systematic and functional manner. Keep in mind that discussion of these entities could easily fill a whole book. The Further Reading list at the back of this book lists source material for those curious to learn more.

Human Rights and Women's Rights

All offices and staff of the UN and its peacekeeping operations are responsible for adhering to international human rights law and reporting possible breaches of it to the proper authorities, but several have a special responsibility for rights. As noted in chapter 12, the Human Rights Council is now the main body for making policy and providing a forum for discussion. Periodically the UN identifies groups that merit attention because their rights have been abridged. For example, in 1997 the secretary-general appointed a distinguished Ugandan diplomat, Olara Otunnu, as special representative for children in armed conflict—in other words, as an advocate for child soldiers. Again, in 1993, the UN launched the International Year of the World's Indigenous People as a way of calling attention to the rights (and other needs) of groups like India's Tribals and Peru's Indians, who have suffered various forms of social, economic, and legal discrimination. Often these "Year of . . ." events lead to follow-up activities that may produce international treaties.

Gender has become an important part of discussions about social and economic development. The Millennium Development Goals (MDGs) promulgated in 2000 (see p. 181) include one specifically addressing gender equality and the empowerment of women as well as another concerning maternal health. The position of women has taken a central place in understanding how and why poor societies do or do not become more affluent and stable. Kofi Annan placed great emphasis on the functional connection between social development and the exercise of basic civil and human rights by women. Many experts argue that society benefits greatly when women can take control of their work, property, and bodies. The UN's effort to publicize women's issues has contributed to a growing international consensus among experts that rights are good for everyone.

For women, as with anyone else, the exercise of rights begins with an understanding of what "rights" are. The Preamble to the Universal Declaration specifies gender equality as a basic right. Even before the Declaration was finished, the UN had established the Commission on the Status of Women, which meets regularly and makes recommendations and suggests international legislation about women's rights. The UN's impact also comes through its public awareness campaigns and its major conferences. Soon after the surfacing of the women's movement during the late 1960s and early 1970s, the UN declared 1975 to be International Women's Year and 1976–1985 the UN Decade for Women. The momentum generated by these efforts led to adoption in 1979 of the Convention on the Elimination of All Forms of Discrimination against Women (CEDAW), described as both "an international bill of rights for women" and "a blueprint for action by countries to guarantee those rights."

Complementing these public relations measures, the UN convened the first global conference on women (in Mexico City), followed by world conferences in Copenhagen (1980), Nairobi (1985), and Beijing (1995). A major purpose of the conference is to agree on a set of shared principles or an agenda for action (a "platform for action") for the years until the next major conference. The conference produced the Beijing Declaration and Platform for Action. Five years later, the General Assembly conducted Beijing +5, a review of the platform.

Fourth World Conference on women opens in Beijing, 1995. UN Photo/Yao Da Wei

LEADING UN ACTORS

Most organizations within the UN system deal with human rights in one way or another, but several have special competence in this area. Note that some of those listed below are not focused fully on human rights but are included here because their goals are closely connected with rights issues.

- The Human Rights Council (www2.ohchr.org/English/bodies/hr council/) was established in 2006 and is based in Geneva, Switzerland. It makes policy, commissions studies, and monitors human rights worldwide. It is the successor to the Commission on Human Rights.

- The Office of the High Commissioner for Human Rights (OHCHR, www.ohchr.org), created in 1993, is based in Geneva, Switzerland. The OHCHR has principal responsibility for UN human rights activities. It has staff in about thirty countries who provide technical services, monitor rights, and investigate alleged rights abuses (more than 100,000 annually).

- The Commission on the Status of Women (www.un.org/women watch/daw/csw), established in 1946, is based in New York. The commission promotes the implementation of equal rights for women and men. It consists of one representative from each of the forty-five member states elected by ECOSOC on the basis of equitable geographical distribution.
- The International Research and Training Institute for the Advancement of Women (INSTRAW, www.un-instraw.org), established in 1976, is headquartered in Santo Domingo, Dominican Republic. INSTRAW is an autonomous body of the UN governed by an ECOSOC-appointed eleven-member board of trustees. INSTRAW supports women's full participation in the economic, social, and political spheres through training, research, and information.
- The UN Development Fund for Women (UNIFEM, www.unifem .undp.org), created in 1976, is based in New York and works closely with the UN Development Programme. UNIFEM funds innovative development activities to benefit women, especially in rural areas of the developing world.

The UN to the Rescue

The UN has always regarded disaster aid as one of its primary missions, defining "disaster" in broad terms that range from earthquakes and floods to disease and famine. Humanitarian aid organizations operate in collaboration with the UN Emergency Relief Coordinator and a committee of representatives from UN agencies and major nongovernmental organizations such as the Red Cross.

Which body of the UN responds to a given emergency depends on the nature of the crisis. If food and shelter are needed, the World Food Programme (WFP) might be the lead agency. Although the WFP engages in social and economic development, its main focus is on helping victims of disaster, long-term refugees, and displaced persons. In 2007, the program fed 86.1 million people in more than eighty nations.

World Food Program air drop in Sudan, November 14, 2007. UN Photo/Fred Noy

Often the WFP collaborates with other UN bodies, such as the High Commissioner for Refugees (UNHCR) and the UN Children's Fund (UNICEF), as well as with NGOs that help distribute aid and ensure that it goes where most needed. The UNHCR is charged with helping and protecting refugees, fulfilling this mission so successfully that it received Nobel Peace Prizes in 1954 and 1981. It has developed "quick impact projects," or QIPs, to bridge the gap between emergency assistance for refugees and refugees returning home and longer-term development aid undertaken by other agencies. Typical QIPs rebuild schools, repair roads, or restore water supplies. Media coverage has made the UNHCR's blue plastic tents familiar to Americans as they view events in parts of Africa and elsewhere.

LEADING UN ACTORS

Four organizations are preeminent in the UN's relief efforts:

- The World Food Programme (WFP, www.wfp.org), created in 1963, is headquartered in Rome, Italy. The WFP underwent a major administrative reformation in the 1990s under Catherine Bertini, the

UNHCR provides aid to cyclone victims, May 2008. UN Photo/UNHCR

organization's first American and first woman executive director. The program has been praised by the US government for its lean and cost-effective performance. The United States is typically the WFP's biggest benefactor. In 2007, the WFP had 10,587 employees and made $2.9 billion in direct expenditures.

- The Office of the United Nations High Commissioner for Refugees (UNHCR, www.unhcr.ch), established in 1950, is based in Geneva, Switzerland. Its staff of about 6,300 works in more than 110 countries and looks after nearly thirty-three million people. In 2003, almost all of the $1.18 billion budget came from voluntary donations from governments.
- The United Nations Children's Fund (UNICEF, www.unicef.org), founded in 1946, is headquartered in New York. UNICEF looks after children in need. Its main task is to help children in developing countries achieve their full potential as human beings, which it does by focusing on rights, needs, and opportunities. Its bedrock statement of belief is the Convention on the Rights of the Child

(CRC), ratified by all the world's nations (except the United States and Somalia), which lays out a bill of rights for children. It encourages governments to adopt internationally recognized ethical standards and to go beyond minimal assurances that citizens have the basics to survive. UNICEF has become embedded in the American consciousness through its famous holiday cards. The organization has eight regional offices and 126 country offices, a staff of seven thousand, and an annual budget of $2.4 billion. The US government has invariably been UNICEF's largest single donor.

- The UN Relief and Works Agency for Palestine Refugees in the Near East (UNRWA, www.unrwa.org), founded in 1949, is based in Gaza City, Palestine. Founded to provide emergency humanitarian aid to Palestinians displaced during the creation of the state of Israel, UNRWA has become a permanent social services agency. It provides health, education, and social services to nearly five million registered Palestinian refugees in the Middle East, under the eye of a UN coordinator. In 2008, the largest contributors were the United States, the European Commission, Sweden, the United Kingdom, Norway, and the Netherlands.

Social and Economic Development and MDGs

Globalization has raised our awareness that the level of the wealth among nations differs greatly, for reasons that are often hard to identify. The UN is a big player in development through its programs and agencies, including the World Bank. These bodies have mandates to pay special attention to the poorest nations. There is growing consensus that the old approach to economic development no longer works well. It is not enough just to raise the overall level of economic growth and assume that all boats will be lifted by the rising tide.

Mark Malloch Brown is a former head of the UN Development Programme, one of the leading bodies in the development effort. He emphasizes the need to strengthen the internal capacity of nations rather than trying to insert infrastructure or industry into a nation without taking into account its social and economic context. He cautions that development "is not a linear thing where you see human

Homeless children beg for food in war-torn Sierra Leone, October 5, 2006.
UN Photo/Eric Kanalstein

suffering and you throw money at it and suffering is solved." Under
prodding from Secretary-General Kofi Annan, the UN responded with
the Millennium Summit of 2000, where the world's leaders pledged
to slash by half the general level of world poverty and hunger, by the
year 2015. World leaders reconvened at a follow-up summit in New
York in 2005 to review progress in achieving the eight Millennium
Development Goals:

- Eradicate extreme poverty and hunger
- Achieve universal primary education
- Promote gender equality and empower women
- Reduce child mortality
- Improve maternal health
- Combat HIV/AIDS, malaria, and other diseases
- Ensure environmental sustainability
- Develop a global partnership for development

All members of the UN family are expected to address the MDGs.
The results have been very mixed, however. Although the worldwide

level of poverty has indeed declined, owing to the expanding economies of China and other Asian nations, African nations remain far behind. Aid from developed countries has not been as great as expected, and such problems as war, civil unrest, and corruption hinder progress in many nations, especially those in Africa. The UN's development infrastructure is still needed.

LEADING UN ACTORS

Among the many UN organizations that participate in the global development effort, several are prominent:

- The UN Development Programme (UNDP, www.undp.org), founded in 1945, is based in New York. The UNDP concentrates on four aspects of development: poverty, the environment, jobs, and women. A recent US government report observed that the UNDP gives the United States an "important channel of communication, particularly in countries where the US has no permanent presence." The United States has been the organization's biggest donor.
- The Food and Agriculture Organization (FAO, www.fao.org) has been operating as a specialized UN agency since 1945, first from Washington, DC, and since 1951 from its headquarters in Rome, Italy. Most of the FAO's work relates to agriculture in a direct way, such as providing technical assistance about farming or nutrition. The FAO's statistics on agriculture, forestry, food supplies, nutrition, and fisheries are authoritative and highly regarded. Many countries, including the United States, have applauded the FAO's efforts to protect commercial fisheries from overexploitation by developing an international plan of action. In 1996 it hosted the World Food Summit, where 185 nations issued the Rome Declaration on World Food Security and pledged to cut the number of hungry people in half by 2015. With some 3,600 staff, the FAO had a budget of $929.8 million for the 2008–9 biennium.
- The International Fund for Agricultural Development (IFAD, www.ifad.org), founded in 1977, is a specialized agency of the UN based in Rome, Italy. IFAD is mandated to combat hunger and rural

poverty in developing countries by providing long-term, low-cost loans for projects that improve the nutrition and food supply of small farmers, nomadic herders, landless rural people, poor women, and others. IFAD also encourages other agencies and governments to contribute funds to these projects. The United States is one of the agency's largest contributors.

- The International Labour Organization (ILO, www.ilo.org), created in 1919, is based in Geneva, Switzerland. The ILO formulates international labor standards through conventions and recommendations that establish minimum standards of labor rights, such as the right to organize, bargain collectively, and receive equal opportunity and treatment. It also offers technical assistance in vocational training and rehabilitation, employment policy, labor relations, working conditions, and occupational safety and health. One of the ILO's most important functions is to investigate and report on whether member states are adhering to the labor conventions and treaties they have signed. The United States, which has a permanent seat on the ILO's governing body, considers the organization vital for addressing exploitative child labor. A US government report claims that the programs have "removed tens of thousands of children" in Central America, Bangladesh, Pakistan, and elsewhere "from exploitative work, placed them in schools, and provided their families with alternative income-producing opportunities." On its fiftieth anniversary, in 1969, the ILO received the Nobel Peace Prize.

- The UN Industrial Development Organization (UNIDO, www.unido.org), which became a specialized agency in 1985, is based in Vienna, Austria. UNIDO helps developing nations establish economies that are globally competitive while respecting the natural environment. It mediates communication between business and government and works to encourage entrepreneurship and bring all segments of the population, including women, into the labor force. Its staff of 651 includes engineers, economists, and technology and environment specialists.

- The UN Office for Project Services (UNOPS, www.unops.org) was founded in 1974 and is headquartered in Copenhagen, Denmark.

UNOPS offers technical services and management for developing nations that seek to boost their economic base. Its staff provides a way for all the world's nations to tap into the vast industrial, commercial, and business experience and expertise of the developed nations.

- UN Volunteers (UNV, www.unv.org), established in 1970 as a subsidiary organ of the UN, is based in Bonn, Germany. During nearly forty years, more than thirty thousand professionals have volunteered through the UNV to work on community-based development projects, provide humanitarian aid, and promote human rights. In any given year, the organization deploys about 7,500 specialists and field-workers in 140 countries.

- The UN Center for Human Settlements (Habitat, www.unchs.org), created in 1978, is headquartered in Nairobi, Kenya. Habitat describes itself as promoting "sustainable human settlement development through advocacy, policy formulation, capacity-building, knowledge creation, and the strengthening of partnerships between government and civil society." Its technical programs and projects focus on a wide range of urban issues, including poverty reduction, postdisaster reconstruction, and water management. At Habitat II, the Second UN Conference on Human Settlements (Istanbul, 1996), delegates approved the Habitat Agenda, in which governments committed themselves to the goals of adequate shelter for all and sustainable urban development.

- The World Bank (www.worldbank.org) was established in 1945 with the goal of reducing global poverty by improving the economies of poor nations. The bank makes loans to developing countries amounting to about $25 billion. In recent years the bank has tried to ensure that local organizations and communities are included in projects in order to increase the chances for success. The World Bank consists of five parts, all based in Washington, DC:

  1. The International Bank for Reconstruction and Development began operations in 1946. It offers loans and financial assistance to member states, each of which subscribes an amount of capital

based on its economic strength. Voting power in the governing body is linked to the subscriptions. Most of its funds come from bonds sold in international capital markets. In fiscal year 2003, its loan commitments amounted to $11.2 billion, for ninety-nine new operations in thirty-seven countries.

2. The International Development Association offers affordable financing, known as credits, to countries with low annual per capita incomes. Most of the funds come from the governments of richer nations. The association lends approximately $7 billion annually.

3. The International Finance Corporation is the developing world's largest multilateral source of loan and equity financing for private-sector projects. The corporation encourages the growth of productive business and efficient capital markets and invests only when it sees an opportunity to complement the role of private investors.

4. The Multilateral Investment Guarantee Agency provides guarantees (that is, insurance) to foreign investors in developing countries. The guarantees protect against losses from political and other factors such as expropriation and war.

5. The International Center for Settlement of Investment Disputes provides arbitration or conciliation services in disputes between governments and private foreign investors.

- The World Health Organization (WHO, www.who.int), founded in 1948, is based in Geneva, Switzerland. One of the largest specialized agencies, with a staff of about eight thousand and an annual budget of approximately $470 million, WHO is charged with improving health and with the eradication or control of diseases. Probably the organization's best-known success is the eradication of smallpox in 1980. WHO has been addressing such other destructive infectious diseases as tuberculosis, malaria, HIV/AIDS, and polio. With six other UN agencies, WHO belongs to the Joint United Nations Programme on HIV/AIDS, described as "the leading advocate for a worldwide response aimed at preventing transmission, providing

AIDS ribbon on UN headquarters building, June 23, 2001. UN Photo/Eskinder Debebe

care and support, reducing the vulnerability of individuals and communities, and alleviating the impact of the epidemic." From 1980 through 1995, WHO collaborated with UNICEF in a campaign to immunize against polio, tetanus, measles, whooping cough, diphtheria, and tuberculosis. In 1999 it received startup funding from the Bill and Melinda Gates Foundation to establish the Global Alliance for Vaccines and Immunization, which is providing immunization against two major killers, hepatitis B and haemophilus influenzae type B.

Protecting the Biosphere

Concern for the natural environment has moved up on everyone's agenda over the past three decades as rapid population increases and economic development have strained the world's forests, farmlands, atmosphere, rivers, and oceans. Climate change is another big concern, as noted in chapter 11. These are areas where the UN's global reach and ability to act as an honest broker has produced impressive results. For example, in response to clear scientific evidence that certain manufactured chemicals, especially chlorofluorocarbons (CFCs), can catalyze the breakdown of ozone in the upper atmosphere and thus increase the amount of harmful ultraviolet sunlight reaching earth, the world community took decisive action under the leadership of the United Nations Environment Programme (UNEP). Following the terms of the 1987 Montreal Protocol, the industrialized countries banned production of CFCs beginning in 1996, while developing countries were granted a grace period for compliance. All signs indicate that the plans are helping to avert an environmental and human catastrophe.

Plants and animals suffer not only through loss of habitat but through direct human exploitation. Some thirty years ago concern over the growing trade in rare birds, reptiles, fish, and mammals led the UN to create the Convention on International Trade in Endangered Species, which is administered by UNEP. This convention has served as a weapon in the fight against poachers, such as those who kill elephants for their tusks, rhinoceroses for their horns, or small mammals for their furs.

LEADING UN ACTORS

Many UN organizations participate in projects or programs that include an environmental aspect; one of them focuses solely on environmental issues.

- The United Nations Environment Programme (UNEP, www.unep .org), founded in 1972, is based in Nairobi, Kenya. A US government report in 2000 credits UNEP with setting the world's environmental agenda, promoting the environmental dimension of sustainable development, and being an authoritative advocate of the global environment. The US government values UNEP's function as a global catalyst of ideas and action and has been the program's biggest donor from the beginning.

- The United Nations Educational, Scientific, and Cultural Organization (UNESCO, www.unesco.org), founded in 1946, is based in Paris, France. UNESCO has a varied mission involving education, research, and public outreach in the sciences, culture, and communications. With a staff of 2,160, it includes 191 national commissions and some 3,600 UNESCO associations, centers, and clubs. In recent years, the US government has strongly supported UNESCO programs for the free flow of ideas, open access to education, the transfer of scientific knowledge, and the protection of cultural and natural heritages.
- The World Meteorological Organization (WMO, www.wmo.ch), founded in 1951, is based in Geneva, Switzerland. The WMO is a specialized agency that provides current scientific information about the atmosphere, freshwaters, and climate. Depletion of the ozone layer, global warming, floods and droughts, and El Niño are among the concerns it addresses. Its staff of more than two hundred serves 182 member states and six territories.

Nuclear, Biological, and Other Threats

The UN has long been a forum for talks about arms control and disarmament, and some of these discussions have produced solid results. Aside from issues of nuclear proliferation, discussed earlier, the UN has sponsored negotiations that have led to such major agreements as treaties outlawing chemical (1992) and bacteriological weapons (1972) and the placement of nuclear weapons on the seabed (1971) or in outer space (1967). Equally important, the UN has helped establish methods to control weapons of mass destruction. The International Atomic Energy Agency, for example, has set up a system of nuclear safeguards and verification, and the Organization for the Prohibition of Chemical Weapons monitors compliance with the Convention on Chemical Weapons.

Secretary-General Ban Ki-moon confers with Mohamed ElBaradei, director-general of the IAEA, April 27, 2008. UN Photo/Mark Garten

LEADING UN ACTORS

Of the three UN bodies responsible for overseeing nuclear, biological, and chemical threats, the International Atomic Energy Agency is best known to the public, owing to its monitoring of the nuclear arms potential of Iran and North Korea.

- The International Atomic Energy Agency (IAEA, www.iaea.org) was established in 1957 and is based in Vienna, Austria. An independent intergovernmental agency, the IAEA helps coordinate the fields of nuclear science and engineering and eases the transfer of technology among nations. Safety and the protection of people against excessive exposure to radiation have also been important concerns. The organization is well recognized as the watchdog for international treaties aimed at containing the unauthorized spread or distribution of nuclear weapons or materials. Its inspectors watch more than a thousand nuclear installations worldwide that are covered under the IAEA Safeguards Programme. The US government strongly endorses the work of the agency and typically provides more than one quarter of the agency's annual budget. The IAEA and its director, Mohamed ElBaradei, shared the Nobel Peace Prize in 2005.

- The Organization for the Prohibition of Chemical Weapons (OPCW, www.opcw.org) is headquartered at The Hague, Netherlands. The primary task of the OPCW is to monitor the provisions of the Convention on the Prohibition of the Development, Production, Stockpiling, and Use of Chemical Weapons and on Their Destruction, which entered into force in 1997. It is the first multilateral disarmament and nonproliferation agreement that addresses the verifiable, worldwide elimination of a whole class of weapons of mass destruction.

- The Preparatory Commission for the Comprehensive Nuclear-Test-Ban Treaty Organization (CTBTO, www.ctbto.org), established in 1996, is based in Vienna, Austria. The commission's main job is to refine a verification plan to ensure that the signers of the Nuclear-Test-Ban Treaty are adhering to its terms.

Guiding Globalization: How the UN Helps Make Things Work

Free markets work best when they have strong government underpinnings, but no one government is in charge of global markets. This is where the UN has become valuable as a monitor, administrator, and facilitator of the many "soft infrastructures" that enable complex international financial and industrial markets to work reasonably well most of the time. The UN has also provided vital aid to governments trying to cope with the fast pace and intensity of modern economic relations, including the rapid swings in currency and capital that can send a seemingly sound national economy into sudden crisis. The International Monetary Fund (IMF) is a specialized agency that offers capital, fiscal and monetary advice, and policy recommendations to national governments. Unlike the World Bank, the IMF's writ runs to all nations, not just the developing ones. In times of crisis, when a member nation is unable to meet its foreign obligations or its financial system becomes unstable, the IMF can offer essential aid in the form of large loans.

For every piece of machinery, every length of fiber-optic cable, every chemical reagent, there has to be a technical standard that permits the enforcement of consistency and standardization. UN bodies set technical standards for machines and the like, and also for laws, procedures, and other intangible elements of the infrastructure. Soft infrastructure includes the rules and standards for the creation, ownership, and development of intellectual property. Software, songs, and genes can all be regarded as forms of property that have value. And as with any form of property, disputes arise about ownership and use. The World Intellectual Property Organization provides services such as helping nations harmonize their laws and procedures about intellectual property, so that creators in each country can more easily be protected in other countries. It administers eleven treaties that set out internationally agreed rights and common standards, which the signatory states agree to enforce within their own borders.

LEADING UN ACTORS

The following organizations are among those that facilitate globalization.

- The International Monetary Fund (IMF, www.imf.int), established in 1944 at the Bretton Woods Conference, is based in Washington, DC. The IMF facilitates international monetary cooperation and provides loans to member states. The 184 member nations are each represented on the board of governors, which sets policy and has general oversight. Regular operations are managed by a twenty-four-member executive board. Member countries subscribe to the IMF through contributions to the budget and can draw on IMF loans according to the level of their subscription. The IMF publishes two important reports: *World Economic Outlook* and *International Capital Markets*.
- The World Intellectual Property Organization (WIPO, www.wipo.int) was founded in 1970 and became a UN specialized agency in

1974. It is based in Geneva, Switzerland. WIPO's mission is to help protect intellectual property worldwide. It raises its annual budget largely through earnings from registration systems.

- The International Civil Aviation Organization (ICAO, www.icao .int), created in 1944, has been a UN specialized agency since 1947 and is based in Montreal, Canada. ICAO sets the international standards and regulations necessary for the safety and efficiency of air transport. It does this by establishing international standards for aircraft, pilots and flight crews, air traffic controllers, ground and maintenance crews, and security in international airports. The United States, a strong supporter of organization, typically provides one quarter of the annual budget.

- The International Maritime Organization (IMO, www.imo.org), founded in 1959, is headquartered in London, England. The IMO's mandate is to make the process of shipping goods for international trade safer and less likely to pollute the seas. Through its meetings, forty conventions, and one thousand codes and recommendations, the IMO has helped develop common standards of safety and efficiency in navigation, technical regulations and practices, and pollution control. The IMO founded the World Maritime University in 1983 in Sweden and has also established the IMO International Maritime Law Institute and the IMO International Maritime Academy.

- The International Telecommunication Union (ITU, www.itu.int), founded in 1865 in Paris as the International Telegraph Union, became the ITU in 1934. It became a UN specialized agency in 1947 and is located in Geneva, Switzerland. The ITU helps governments and the private sector coordinate and improve global telecommunication networks and services. The staff of some 740 also offers technical assistance to developing countries.

- The Universal Postal Union (UPU, www.upu.int), established in the Berne Treaty of 1874, became a UN specialized agency in 1948. It is headquartered in Bern, Switzerland. The UPU regulates and facilitates cooperation among international postal services, as well as providing advice, mediation, and technical assistance. The Universal Postal Congress meets every five years.

Drug Trafficking

"Growing evidence suggests that drug abuse is being brought under control" is the good news from the executive director of the UN Office on Drugs and Crime (UNODC). The agency's 2007 *World Drug Report* shows that global markets for illicit drugs remained largely stable in 2005–6 but that opium production in Afghanistan remained a major problem. Detailed and authoritative reports such as this provide vital information to the world's illicit drug experts, policymakers, and enforcement officials.

The rapid growth of the international narcotics trade has led the UN to coordinate its antidrug resources under the UNODC, established in 1997. The governing body of the UNDCP (UN International Drug Control Programme) is the Commission on Narcotic Drugs (CND), a functional commission of ECOSOC and the UN's main source of drug-related policy. Three international conventions form the basis for the CND's policies: the Single Convention on Narcotic Drugs (1961), which tries to confine drugs to medical use only; the Convention on Psychotropic Substances (1971), which seeks to control synthetic drugs; and the UN Convention against Illicit Traffic in Narcotic Drugs and Psychotropic Substances (1988), which deals mainly with drug trafficking and related issues like money laundering. However, the CND does not actually monitor implementation of these treaties. That task is the responsibility of the International Narcotics Control Board, an independent panel of thirteen persons elected by ECOSOC and financed by the UN.

Among UNODC's major efforts are the Global Assessment Programme, which provides accurate information about the international drug problem; the legal Advisory Program, which assists governments in writing laws against the drug trade and helps train judicial officials; and the Illicit Crop Monitoring Programme. The Alternative Development Programme tries to nip the drug problem at its source by offering farmers alternative crops that will enable them to earn a decent, and legal, living.

One UN plan has been to identify the nations that are the largest

UNODC vocational training program in Afghanistan, May 22, 2006. UN Photo/Eskinder Debebe

producers of opium and strongly encourage them to take action. That has put the spotlight on Afghanistan, which has been the world's largest opium producer in most recent years. Former US permanent representative to the UN Zalmay Khalilzad was ambassador to Afghanistan in 2003–5 and knows the problem firsthand. He fears that the drug trade may criminalize the political system and the economy. "As long as there is demand for narcotics someone will produce them if the price is high enough, but in Afghanistan there is the issue of the right combination of alternative livelihoods with attacks against labs, eradication of large fields, and law enforcement going after traffickers and people in government who maybe are working with traffickers." The Afghan government has committed itself to a strong antidrug, anti–poppy growing policy. All nations have an interest in the fate of Afghanistan's poppy fields, and the UN has begun aligning its bodies to act effectively. Among other things, the UN has reestablished its UNDCP Afghanistan office.

LEADING UN ACTORS

Three bodies oversee most of the UN's fight against the trade in illegal drugs.

- The UN Office on Drugs and Crime (UNODC, www.unodc.org), established in 1997, is based in Vienna, Austria. The UNODC has two components, the Crime Programme and the Drug Programme (formally known as the UN Drug Control Programme, or UNDCP). Through the Drug Programme, the UNODC offers an integrated approach that begins with the farmer and ends with the drug dealer and money launderer. The UNDCP also monitors implementation of drug-related decisions by ECOSOC and other UN bodies. The Crime Programme focuses on corruption, organized crime, trafficking in human beings, and terrorism. The Drug Programme compiles and disseminates information about illicit drugs, monitors illegal drug-related agriculture, fights the laundering of drug-related money, seeks alternative crops for farmers in drug-growing regions, and helps governments write antidrug legislation. The UNODC has some five hundred staff members and twenty-two field offices. Most of its funding comes from voluntary contributions by member states.
- The Commission on Narcotic Drugs (CND, www. uncnd.org) was established in 1946 and has its headquarters in Vienna, Austria.

    The CND makes UN policy about drugs and is the governing body for the UN Drug Control Programme. It is a functional commission of ECOSOC.
- The International Narcotics Control Board (INCB, www.incb.org) was created in 1968 and is located in Vienna, Austria. The INCB is an independent body, funded by the UN, that monitors compliance with the three international conventions on narcotics and drug trafficking.

CHAPTER 16

Stars in the UN Firmament

The United Nations of the 21st century can attain its goals only by working with partners.

—Ban Ki-moon, secretary-general of the United Nations

Aside from the UN secretary-general, some of the heads of UN agencies and commissions have shone brightly in their public careers. Former deputy secretary-general Mark Malloch Brown was recently made a British lord and became his country's minister for Africa, Asia, and the UN. Mohamed ElBaradei of the IAEA was corecipient of the Nobel Peace Prize in 2005. But there are also other kinds of stars— some more comfortable before a camera or a theater audience, some at home in the corporate boardroom—who have aligned themselves with the UN.

Peace Messengers and Goodwill Ambassadors

The UN's most visible and glamorous supporters are probably the dozens of actors, athletes, and other celebrities who have become official goodwill ambassadors, peace ambassadors, and peace messengers. On

Actor George Clooney, a UN messenger for peace, with Indian peacekeepers in the Democratic Republic of Congo DRC, January 25, 2008. UN Photo/ Marie Frechon

their own time they volunteer to travel the world, representing the UN before every imaginable kind of audience and spreading word of its programs and concerns. Some of these celebrity volunteers serve at large and represent the UN as a whole, while others sign on with a part of the system like the UN Development Programme, the UN Population Fund, or UNICEF. Actor Danny Kaye became the first goodwill ambassador in 1953, with UNICEF, and Audrey Hepburn joined shortly afterward. Soon there were many more: actor Peter Ustinov, singers Harry Belafonte and Judy Collins, and actress Vanessa Redgrave. Today, Angelina Jolie is working to help refugees while Nicole Kidman campaigns on behalf of women's empowerment. High-profile helpers come from everywhere: from China, singer Leon Lai; from Italy, actors Lino Banfi and Simona Marchini; from Greece, singer Nana Mouskouri; from Portugal, actress Catarina Furtado; and from Switzerland, Roger Federer.

UN Messengers of Peace

Princess Haya Bint Al Hussein	Michael Douglas
Daniel Barenboim	Jane Goodall
George Clooney	Yo-Yo Ma
Paulo Coelho	Elie Wiesel
Midori Goto	

Peace ambassador the late opera star Luciano Pavarotti raised money for the UN's refugee agency, including some $2 million at one event for Angolan refugees. Actor Danny Glover has toured widely in Africa promoting development, and actress Mia Farrow, a UNICEF goodwill peace ambassador, has campaigned for polio immunization and international aid for Darfur.

The United Nations Foundation

On September 18, 1997, businessman and philanthropist Ted Turner made an unprecedented gesture when he announced a $1 billion gift in support of UN causes. His historic donation was made in the form of Time-Warner stock, given in ten annual installments. In response to Turner's gift, the UN Foundation (UNF) was created with the goal of "promoting a more peaceful, prosperous, and just world," which it seeks by publicizing and funding various UN activities. Its four main functions are to (1) provide additional funding for programs and people served by UN agencies; (2) forge new partnerships between UN agencies, the private sector, and nongovernmental organizations to improve support for the UN while enhancing the effectiveness of service delivery; (3) in cooperation with a sister organization, the Better World Fund, sponsor or conduct efforts aimed at educating the public about the UN's unique role in addressing global issues; and (4) encourage public and private donors to help demonstrate what the UN and the world can do when the public and private sectors cooperate and coinvest.

Actress Nicole Kidman at UNIFEM press conference for campaign "Say No to Violence against Women," April 22, 2008. UN Photo/Devra Berkowitz

At the foundation's tenth anniversary in 2007, Secretary-General Ban Ki-moon praised the organization for being the UN's "best friend." He continued, "You have grown into a tireless advocate for the United Nations, helping to tell our story and strengthen our relationship with the United States. You have supported our capacity to respond to global challenges, in a world where no sector and no country can address these challenges alone."

An example of how these goals play out in the real world can be seen in the Adopt-A-Minefield campaign. In many parts of the world, the land is sewn with small land mines, relics of civil wars and other violent outbreaks that remain lethal to humans long after the fighting has ended. The mines are invisible, and their locations are seldom known with accuracy. The UN agency most involved in clearing mines is the UNDP, which has collaborated with the Better World Fund and the UNA-USA (see below) to sponsor Adopt-A-Minefield, enabling companies or individuals to pay for mine removal in more than one hundred locations. Costs vary considerably, from $27,000 to clear a village of land mines in Croatia to $34,000 for a field in Cambodia.

Other UN-Oriented Organizations

The United Nations Association of the United States of America (UNA-USA) is a nonpartisan, nonprofit group consisting of some twenty-three thousand Americans. The nation's largest grassroots foreign policy organization, it seeks to educate Americans about the issues facing the UN and to encourage support for strong US leadership in the UN. It is a leading center of policy research on the UN and generally promotes participation in global issues. It offers forums and seminars about major international issues and helps coordinate the Model United Nations (see appendix D), an innovative simulation in which students act the roles of diplomats. It also reaches out to the business community through its Business Council for the United Nations. The headquarters of UNA-USA is in New York, with chapters in more than a hundred other cities. The organization can be reached at its web site (www.unausa.org) or by phone (212.907.1300).

UNA-USA offers an interesting twist on the Model UN concept, described below. The Global Classrooms program brings simulation of a General Assembly session into the classroom through curriculum units designed for grades seven through twelve. The curriculum materials include a teacher's guide and an accompanying student workbook.

UNA-USA belongs to a global network of associations, the World Federation of United Nations Associations (WFUNA), which was established in 1946 as a "peoples' movement" for the UN. The federation has more than a hundred member associations. Every three years representatives of the national associations meet in a plenary assembly, which elects the leadership positions and identifies high-priority issues of concern to the world community.

Other UN Friends

The Business Council for the United Nations (BCUN) reaches out to the private sector through meetings and partnerships. Through the

BCUN, business owners and managers learn about the UN and world issues, and gain access to the largest diplomatic community in the world. The council cites its value in promoting investment flow to the developing world and helping to bridge the "digital divide."

The Academic Council on the United Nations System (ACUNS, www .acuns.wlu.ca) is another UN-focused organization, created to encourage education, writing, and research that contribute to the understanding of international issues and promotion of global cooperation. A primary goal is to strengthen the study of international organizations and to foster ties among academics, the UN system, and international organizations. The ACUNS was created in 1987 at Dartmouth College as an international association of scholars, teachers, practitioners, and others who study or are active in the United Nations system and international organizations. Ongoing projects include research and policy workshops, an annual meeting about UN and international issues, a summer workshop for younger scholars and practitioners hosted in cooperation with the American Society for International Law (ASIL), and a dissertation awards program. The organization also cosponsors an email discussion listserv with the International Organization section of the International Studies Association (ISA).

Model UN

Probably the best-known program about the UN is the Model United Nations, which is a simulation of the General Assembly and other bodies (see appendix D). This program catapults students into the world of diplomacy and negotiation, encouraging them to "step into the shoes of ambassadors from U.N. member states to debate current issues on the organization's vast agenda." Playing the role of delegates, students draft resolutions, "negotiate with supporters and adversaries, resolve conflicts, and navigate the U.N.'s rules of procedures," with the goal of focusing "international cooperation" to solve problems that affect almost every country on earth.

Most Model UN programs are offered at colleges and universities, though some are held in middle schools and high schools. They are popular not only in the United States but in countries around the

Model UN Session in General Assembly hall, 2008. National Model UN (NMUN)

world. A calendar of Model UN events is available on the UNA-USA web site. Model UN meetings can be very, very big, even into the thousands. Perhaps the largest is the National Model UN (NMUN) held annually in New York, which seeks to draw participants from around the country. The American Model UN (AMUN) meeting held in Chicago also attracts very large attendance.

Partnership with NGOs

The UN's Department of Public Information (DPI) is charged with reaching people around the world and helping them better understand the work and aims of the UN. It has established working relationships with nearly 1,500 nongovernmental organizations around the globe that have strong information programs. It is a mutually rewarding relationship. The DPI provides NGOs with timely and accurate information about the UN, and the NGOs disseminate the information to their constituencies.

CHAPTER 17

The Coup against Boutros Boutros-Ghali

Every country probably trashed us. I guess they didn't like the way we did it, but there was no other way. We tried to do it more subtly, we tried to ask Boutros to step down. He had promised he was a one-term, and he reneged on that promise. It got uglier and uglier, so we finally decided to stick to our guns.
—Michael Sheehan, former US National Security Council
staff member, 1995–97

If you think the US government is at the mercy of the UN or that the UN can dictate policy to the United States, consider the case of Boutros Boutros-Ghali, who was Kofi Annan's predecessor as secretary-general. Boutros-Ghali served one term, from 1992 to 1997, and declared his intention to run for another. But he never made it, because, to put it bluntly, he fell afoul of key US diplomats and political leaders, who blocked him through a carefully staged coup. The coup is no secret. Boutros-Ghali has described his experiences in writing, and many participants and observers have offered their own contributions. The story merits a brief retelling as an example of the fine line that the secretary-general has to walk in threading a path to successful leadership.

Boutros-Ghali's downfall had two main roots. One of them was the disaffection of his middle managers, who did not lift a finger to defend him when the Americans and their accomplices made their move. Longtime UN insider Mark Malloch Brown blames Boutros-Ghali's background as a senior official in the Egyptian government for giving him an exalted view of his office, which was exactly the wrong thing to emulate as secretary-general. Instead of making himself indispensable by helping nations solve problems, too many saw him as doing "the diplomatic equivalent of stamping his foot while simultaneously staring down his nose. It didn't make most heads of state and foreign ministers particularly want to work with him."

A highly placed UN insider confirms this picture of an arrogant, isolated secretary-general. "The thing about Boutros that we were most unhappy about as staff was he didn't really like the institution that he headed. He was completely aloof and detached from all of us." His bullying caused the staff to either remain silent or tell him what he wanted to hear, which meant that "he was no longer getting the best opinions from people." His manner of working, says the insider, "was hopeless." He would leave managers out of the loop, presenting them with constant administrative and policy surprises. They would often find an ambassador or minister coming to them and saying, "As your boss said the other day" or "As we said to your boss the other day," and they hadn't even been given a copy of the notes on the meeting. "That was really bad for efficiency and for morale."

The Secretariat's staff had to endure these indignities, but not the United States. Once Boutros-Ghali got on the bad side of US permanent representative Madeleine Albright, it was all downhill. "Personal dislike was a real issue on policy," says the insider. "In the case of Boutros and Madeleine, he didn't like her style, she didn't like his nature, and their dislike coincided with the fact that professionally they didn't see eye to eye."

Early in 1996 Albright became leader of an American effort to prevent Boutros-Ghali from seeking a second term. It was a period of strained relations between the UN and the United States, owing to a string of failed operations (fighting in Somalia and genocidal massacres in Rwanda and Srebrenica). Michael Sheehan, who was a National Security Council staff member at the time, recalls that he found himself one of the initial conspirators. "We got together and said Boutros needs to go, he is not good for the UN, and he's not good for the US, and not good for the US and the UN."

The conspirators quickly discovered that even though Boutros-Ghali had little solid support in the UN, they had greatly underestimated his determination to run for a second term and his skill in marshaling support. He used "every trick he knew, with very subtle and not so subtle promises and threats to countries. No one wanted to oppose him." "We ended up standing alone in broad daylight," reflects Sheehan, "instead of slipping it to him." The deed would have to be done publicly, in the modern-day equivalent of the Roman forum.

The conspirators acted with growing support from President Bill Clinton and Secretary of State Warren Christopher, who were put off by Boutros-Ghali's lobbying of member states. "They recognized that he forgot what his job was," Sheehan says. "He was a servant of the member states, a servant for the organization, not an entity unto himself." Realizing that they needed to have an appealing alternative candidate, the coup team wrote a memo to Clinton in spring 1996 offering three candidates—Lakhdar Brahimi, Olara Otunnu, and Kofi Annan—each of whom was from a nation in Africa. Sheehan favored Annan or Brahimi. "I had been working for both of them and I loved both of them. At the time I didn't know Otunnu, who was being pushed by another member of the NSC staff. The president approved this strategy and said that, yes, he needs to go, that sounds good. We also discussed the Asian option and others, but we thought the post was going to stay in Africa."

When the Americans began looking for votes in the General Assembly, they discovered that Annan seemed to have the strongest support, so he became the lead candidate. "The French extracted a promise from us to support them to get the post of under-secretary for peacekeeping, which we granted. And that was the deal. Kofi Annan became secretary-general to the delight of everyone." Actually, much of the "delight" was after the fact. Sheehan recalls that after the vote, mass amnesia struck, and "it was like rats off a sinking ship." "Now

Secretary-General Boutros Boutros-Ghali addresses the General Assembly, December 10, 1996. UN DPI Photo/ Evan Schneider

everyone supported Annan from day one, so he was the choice. I remember differently. We were under enormous pressure to cut a deal, particularly from [French president Jacques] Chirac and [South Africa's] Nelson Mandela, who called the president on many occasions to lobby for Boutros-Ghali. I never felt more pressure from anything I ever did during five years in the White House. It was hard." Sheehan praises Albright for not bending to pressures on Boutros-Ghali's behalf. "It wouldn't have happened without her. She hung in there. It was the right thing to do."

The coup raises the question of whether a single nation, no matter how dominant, should be able to decide that it doesn't like the secretary-general and methodically force him out. Our UN insider has no problem with that, though faulting the reasons offered by the US government. "The Americans were right to get rid of Boutros but not on the ground that he wasn't reforming the UN. The official reason they gave was that he was resistant to reform, which was nonsense. In fact he did want reform more than anyone else. He may have done it in a way that we, the staff, didn't like, but he decisively slashed posts, slashed high-level functions, really did reform."

The real reason for Boutros-Ghali's ouster, the insider claims, was that he became a political liability in the US presidential election of 1996. "He let the Republicans have a useful piece of ammunition: they said if there's a Republican president, we would not allow our foreign policy to be made by an un-elected Egyptian bureaucrat sitting in New York. Of course he wasn't making policy. Of course the Americans could do what they want with Boutros. But perception was bad enough politically for Clinton because what mattered was what people thought the truth was. Clinton was, I think, increasingly convinced that he had to get rid of this liability. Why did he need to give the Republicans a stick to beat him on the head with?"

CHAPTER 18

Making a Career at the UN

We were dealing with actual human beings, and I could put my head to the pillow at night knowing that what I did made a real difference in people's lives—people I could see and feel and meet and touch and actually talk to. That kind of direct connection, that's something that UNHCR affords that's truly extraordinary.

—Shashi Tharoor, former UN under-secretary-general for communications and public information

To put a face on the career UN staffer, it's helpful to listen as one of them talks about his early years in the UN as an idealistic young administrator out to learn about the world. Shashi Tharoor was born in India, educated there and in the United States, and in 1978 became a staff member of the UN High Commissioner for Refugees (UNHCR), which assists refugees in resettling. He was posted to Singapore from 1981 to 1984 to help organize efforts to aid the thousands of Vietnamese fleeing their homeland in the aftermath of the collapse of the Saigon government and the takeover of the country by the communists in 1975. From 1989 to 1996, Tharoor was part of the peacekeeping office of the Secretariat as a special assistant to the under-secretary-

Under-Secretary-General Shashi Tharoor addresses United Nations Forum
on the information age, November 29, 2006. UN Photo/Paulo Filgueiras

general for peacekeeping operations. In 2002 he became under-
secretary-general for communications and public information, and in
2006 he made an unsuccessful bid to succeed Kofi Annan as secretary-
general. In an interview at his UN office in 2002, Tharoor recalled his
challenging work as a new staff member of the UNHCR:

"The High Commissioner for Refugees was a great place to begin
my career because it really attracts a lot of idealists, in those days in
particular. What really brought me to a conviction of the indispensability of the UN was working for UNHCR in the field. I arrived in
Singapore at the peak of the Vietnamese boat-people crisis. There
were four thousand refugees living at the camp, sleeping twenty-five,
thirty to a room this size. The situation had become totally unmanage-
able. When refugees left Vietnam by boat, they were picked up by
boats sailing into Singapore. The Singapore government was very
unhappy about having refugees come in, and they manifested this by
making difficult the disembarkation of some of these refugees and

having nothing to do with the camps themselves. Other countries who were receiving Vietnamese refugees ran their own camps, usually with their military, whereas in Singapore the UN was asked to run their camps.

"UNHCR in those days believed it was not an operational agency, so we weren't supposed to be running camps. It was an extraordinary challenge for someone who was in their twenties as I was. I essentially invented operational partners by going to churches and church groups and saying, 'Put your label on us and say you're the operational partner, and I will raise money to get the staff and we will run the camp.' I got volunteers from the city, including wives of diplomats, to come in and teach refugees and run camps. I took donations from the community for the benefit of the refugees. I got refugees to run their own democracy, elect their own camp leader.

"On the diplomatic side, there was dealing with a tough government, trying to use the power of my office to get them to cooperate. Church groups can go and help refugees, volunteers can go and help refugees, but only the UN can go to a government. I would tell officials, 'You have an obligation to honor your international commitment to this organization.' Even if they're not signatories to the UN convention, as a member of the General Assembly they're bound by the statute of the organization, which is a General Assembly resolution. We expect them to honor their role as a government and a member of the UN.

"We had to invent whole new procedures. For example when ships came in, [the authorities] insisted that every ship that had refugees had to provide a guarantee that the refugees would be resettled. Then they realized that some of the guarantees were worthless because some of the ships were from Bangladesh and India and flag-of-convenience ships flying the Liberian flag or the Panamanian flag. What use was a letter of guarantee from Liberia that they will resettle their refugees?

"The Singaporeans then wanted a letter from a country of resettlement. We had to invent a scheme, where we had looked into the ownership of a ship, and got a country of registration to actually provide the guarantees, and then there were the weekly meetings in my office with the immigration chiefs of embassies. It's a sobering thought that there are kids growing up French, or Canadian, or American today because of my skill or lack thereof in persuading an immigration officer to bend the rules.

"Every month more were arriving, I would imagine somewhere between twelve thousand and twenty thousand refugees passed through my hands in Singapore. In one case, for example, a family left for Singapore on a tiny boat with a cannibalized tractor engine. It wasn't a proper motor, and sure enough it conked out and they were drifting on the high seas. They ran out of food, out of water, and they were subsisting on rainwater and hope. What do the parents do? They slit their fingers to get their babies to suck their own blood in order to survive. They were finally rescued by an American ship, and they were so weak they couldn't stand up; they had to be lifted out of the boat. We rushed them into intensive care in the hospital as soon as we could disembark them. Now, to see that same family three or four months later, healthy, well fed, well rested, well dressed, heading off to new lives in the United States, there is simply no job that could compare with that sort of thing—pure human satisfaction.

"When Poland declared martial law in December 1981, do you remember the Solidarity movement [labor union] and all of that? A Polish ship docked in Singapore on a Saturday, and four or five Polish seamen jumped ship and looked up the UN in the phone book and came to my office and wanted asylum. I had no authority to grant asylum. I woke up the director of international protections of the UNHCR and said, 'What do I do?' The guy said, 'Follow the convention, interview these people, and determine if in your view they should have refugee status. If you do, they are refugees.'

"It was quite a drama. I interviewed them. I felt that they had a credible case. They said they were supporters of Solidarity and if they went back they would be locked up, so they jumped ship. I said, 'I recognize you as refugees,' and basically said to the Singaporeans, 'You've got to let these people stay.' The Singaporeans were furious, but I contacted some embassies and said, 'Could you try and take these people?' We worked out a scheme. The Singaporeans retaliated by banning shore leave for all Polish seamen. They kept saying, 'You are only here to look after the Vietnamese.' And I said, 'No, I'm with the UN High Commissioner for Refugees. Vietnamese happen to be my caseload, but anybody else who comes in, I'm legally mandated under the statute of the office to help them.'

"A couple of months after this first episode, I got a frantic call from the Singaporeans and the Americans, one after the other. A Polish sailor had jumped ship and swum to an American destroyer in the port. Singapore naval police and immigration police said he had to be handed over because he was illegal. The American captain said that the sailor was fleeing communism and he would not surrender him. There was a diplomatic standoff. Neither side wanted this to hit the press, but the Singaporeans wouldn't let the American ship sail with the Polish seaman on board, and the Polish seaman couldn't go back to his ship. The Americans allowed the Singaporeans to take him off the ship under the condition that he be brought to me. He was brought to the US consul's office in the embassy, where it was determined he had refugee status, at which point we took charge and put him in a little hotel in Singapore (where it's not an inexpensive proposition for the UN, I can tell you).

"Then I started putting heat on the Americans, saying, 'Take him because we solved the problem for you and you have to resettle him.' It dragged on for a couple of months before the United States agreed to take him. A new consul arrived and was very helpful and said that he would take charge.

"I got a lovely postcard from San Diego from this Polish seaman, saying, 'I never will forget you, Mr. Shashi.' One of the precious souvenirs of my career!

"Singapore was such an extraordinary period, and among other things it convinced me about the indispensability of the UN cause. Most things I've done under the UN, only the UN could have done. The UN has a hell of a lot of advantages in dealing with authorities. There are so many stories in which the governmental influence that the UN can bring to bear changes the lives and fortunes of people who are in danger or distress."

ACABQ—Advisory Committee on Administrative and Budgetary
  Questions
ACUNS—Academic Council on the United Nations System
ASIL—American Society for International Law
BCUN—Business Council for the United Nations
CEDAW—Convention on the Elimination of All Forms of
  Discrimination against Women
CND—Commission on Narcotic Drugs
CONGO—Conference on Non-Governmental Organizations in
  Consultative Status
CRC—Convention on the Rights of the Child
CTBTO—Preparatory Commission for the Comprehensive Nuclear
  Test-Ban Treaty Organization
DPA—Department of Political Affairs
DPI—Department of Public Information
DPKO—Department of Peacekeeping Operations
E10—Elected ten members of the Security Council
ECOSOC—Economic and Social Council
ECOWAS—Economic Council of West African States

ETTA—East Timor Transitional Administration
EU—European Union
FAO—Food and Agriculture Organization
G-77—Group of 77, a coalition of developing countries
GA—General Assembly
GAO—General Accountability Office
GATT—General Agreement on Tariffs and Trade
HCHR—High Commissioner for Human Rights
IAEA—International Atomic Energy Agency
ICAO—International Civil Aviation Organization
ICC—International Criminal Court
ICCPR—International Covenant on Civil and Political Rights
ICJ—International Court of Justice
ICTR—International Criminal Tribunal for Rwanda
ICTY—International Criminal Tribunal for (the former) Yugoslavia
IDA—International Development Association
IFAD—International Fund for Agricultural Development
ILO—International Labor Organization
IMF—International Monetary Fund
IMO—International Maritime Organization
INSTRAW—International Research and Training Institute for the
    Advancement of Women
IPCC—Intergovernmental Panel on Climate Change
ISA—International Studies Association
ITU—International Telecommunications Union
NAM—Nonaligned Movement
NATO—North Atlantic Treaty Organization
NGO—nongovernmental organization
OAU—Organization of African Unity
OEWG—Open-Ended Working Group on the Question of Equitable
    Representation on and Increase in the Membership of the Security
    Council
OHCHR—Office of the High Commissioner for Human Rights
OIOS—Office of Internal Oversight Services
OPCW—Organization for the Prohibition of Chemical Weapons

P5—Permanent 5 members of the Security Council
PCT—Patent Cooperation Treaty
PR—A Nation's Permanent Representative or Perm Rep
SC—Security Council
SG—Secretary General
UN—United Nations
UNA-USA—United Nations Association of the United States of America
UNAIDS—Joint United Nations Program on HIV/AIDS
UNCTAD—UN Conference on Trade and Development
UNDCP—UN International Drug Control Program
UNDP—United Nations Development Program
UNEP—United Nations Environment Program
UNESCO—United Nations Educational, Scientific, and Cultural Organization
UNF—United Nations Foundation
UNFPA—United Nations Population Fund
UNHCR—Office of the United Nations High Commissioner for Refugees
UNICEF—United Nations Children's Fund
UNIDO—UN Industrial Development Organization
UNIFEM—UN Development Fund for Women
UNMEE—UN Mission in Ethiopia and Eritrea
UNMOVIC—United Nations Monitoring, Verification, and Inspection Commission on Iraq
UNODC—United Nations Office on Drugs and Crime
UNOPS—UN Office for Project Services
UNRWA—United Nations Relief and Works Agency for Palestine Refugees in the Near East
UNSCOM—United Nations Special Commission on Iraq
UNTAET—UN Transitional Administration in East Timor
UNTSO—United Nations Truce Supervision Organization
UNV—UN Volunteers
UPU—Universal Postal Union
WEOG—Western Europe and Others Group

WFP—World Food Program
WHO—World Health Organization
WIPO—World Intellectual Property Organization
WMO—World Meteorological Organization

Membership of Principal United Nations Organs

GENERAL ASSEMBLY

The General Assembly is composed of all 192 United Nations Member States. The States, and the dates on which they became members, are listed in appendix C.

SECURITY COUNCIL

The Security Council has fifteen members. The United Nations Charter designates five states as permanent members, and the General Assembly elects ten other members for two-year terms. The term of office for each nonpermanent member of the Council ends on December 31 of the year indicated in parentheses next to its name.

The five permanent members of the Security Council are China, France, the Russian Federation, the United Kingdom, and the United States.

The ten nonpermanent members of the Council in 2008 were Belgium (2008), Burkina Faso (2009), Costa Rica (2009), Croatia (2009), Indonesia (2008), Italy (2008), Libya (2009), Panama (2008), South Africa (2008), and Vietnam (2009).

ECONOMIC AND SOCIAL COUNCIL

The Economic and Social Council has fifty-four members, elected for three-year terms by the General Assembly. The term of office for each member expires on December 31 of the year indicated in parentheses next to its name. In 2007 the Council was composed of the following fifty-four states: Albania (2007), Algeria (2009), Angola (2008), Austria (2008), Barbados (2009), Belarus (2009), Benin (2008), Bolivia (2009), Brazil (2007), Canada (2009), Cape Verde (2009), Chad (2007), China (2007), Costa Rica (2007), Cuba (2008), Czech Republic (2008), Democratic Republic of the Congo (2007), Denmark (2007), El Salvador (2009), France (2008), Germany (2008), Greece (2008), Guinea (2007), Guinea-Bissau (2008), Guyana (2008), Haiti (2008), Iceland (2007), India (2007), Indonesia (2009), Iraq (2009), Japan (2008), Kazakhstan (2009), Lithuania (2007), Luxembourg (2009), Madagascar (2008), Malawi (2009), Mauritania (2008), Mexico (2007), Netherlands (2009), New Zealand (2007), Pakistan (2007), Paraguay (2008), Philippines (2009), Portugal (2007), Romania (2009), Russian Federation (2007), Saudi Arabia (2008), Somalia (2009), South Africa (2007), Sri Lanka (2008), Sudan (2009), Thailand (2007), United Kingdom (2007), and United States (2009).

TRUSTEESHIP COUNCIL

The Trusteeship Council is made up of the five permanent members of the Security Council—China, France, Russian Federation, United Kingdom, and the United States. With the independence of Palau, the last remaining United Nations Trust Territory, the council formally suspended operations on November 1, 1994. The council amended its rules of procedure to drop the obligation to meet annually and agreed to meet as the occasion required: by its decision or the decision of its president or at the request of a majority of its members or the General Assembly or the Security Council.

INTERNATIONAL COURT OF JUSTICE

The International Court of Justice has fifteen members, elected by both the General Assembly and the Security Council. Judges hold nine-year terms, which end February 5 of the year indicated in parentheses next to their name.

The current composition of the court is as follows: Ronny Abraham (France, 2009), Awn Shawkat Al-Khasawneh (Jordan, 2009), Mohamed Bennouna (Morocco, 2015), Thomas Buergenthal (United States, 2015), Rosalyn Higgins (United Kingdom, 2009), Shi Jiuyong (China, 2012), Kenneth Keith (New Zealand, 2015), Abdul Koroma (Sierra Leone, 2012), Hisashi Owada (Japan, 2012), Gonzalo Parra-Aranguren (Venezuela, 2009), Raymond Ranjeva (Madagascar, 2009), Bernardo Sepulveda Amor (Mexico, 2015), Bruno Simma (Germany, 2012), Leonid Skotnikov (Russian Federation, 2015), and Peter Tomka (Slovakia, 2012).

The Universal Declaration of Human Rights

PREAMBLE

Whereas recognition of the inherent dignity and of the equal and inalienable rights of all members of the human family is the foundation of freedom, justice and peace in the world,

Whereas disregard and contempt for human rights have resulted in barbarous acts which have outraged the conscience of mankind, and the advent of a world in which human beings shall enjoy freedom of speech and belief and freedom from fear and want has been proclaimed as the highest aspiration of the common people,

Whereas it is essential, if man is not to be compelled to have recourse, as a last resort, to rebellion against tyranny and oppression, that human rights should be protected by the rule of law,

Whereas it is essential to promote the development of friendly relations between nations,

Whereas the peoples of the United Nations have in the Charter reaffirmed their faith in fundamental human rights, in the dignity and worth of the human person and in the equal rights of men and women and have determined to promote social progress and better standards of life in larger freedom,

Whereas Member States have pledged themselves to achieve, in cooperation with the United Nations, the promotion of universal respect for and observance of human rights and fundamental freedoms,

Whereas a common understanding of these rights and freedoms is of the greatest importance for the full realization of this pledge,

Now, Therefore the general assembly proclaims this universal declaration of human rights as a common standard of achievement for all peoples and all nations, to the end that every individual and every organ of society, keeping this Declaration constantly in mind, shall strive by teaching and education to promote respect for these rights and freedoms and by progressive measures, national and international, to secure their universal and effective recognition and observance, both among the peoples of Member States themselves and among the peoples of territories under their jurisdiction.

Article 1.
All human beings are born free and equal in dignity and rights. They are endowed with reason and conscience and should act towards one another in a spirit of brotherhood.

Article 2.
Everyone is entitled to all the rights and freedoms set forth in this Declaration, without distinction of any kind, such as race, colour, sex, language, religion, political or other opinion, national or social origin, property, birth or other status. Furthermore, no distinction shall be made on the basis of the political, jurisdictional or international status of the country or territory to which a person belongs, whether it be independent, trust, non-self-governing or under any other limitation of sovereignty.

Article 3.
Everyone has the right to life, liberty and security of person.

Article 4.
No one shall be held in slavery or servitude; slavery and the slave trade shall be prohibited in all their forms.

Article 5.
No one shall be subjected to torture or to cruel, inhuman or degrading treatment or punishment.

Article 6.
Everyone has the right to recognition everywhere as a person before the law.

Article 7.
All are equal before the law and are entitled without any discrimination to equal protection of the law. All are entitled to equal protection against any discrimination in violation of this Declaration and against any incitement to such discrimination.

Article 8.
Everyone has the right to an effective remedy by the competent national tribunals for acts violating the fundamental rights granted him by the constitution or by law.

Article 9.
No one shall be subjected to arbitrary arrest, detention or exile.

Article 10.
Everyone is entitled in full equality to a fair and public hearing by an independent and impartial tribunal, in the determination of his rights and obligations and of any criminal charge against him.

Article 11.
(1) Everyone charged with a penal offence has the right to be presumed innocent until proved guilty according to law in a public trial at which he has had all the guarantees necessary for his defence.
(2) No one shall be held guilty of any penal offence on account of any act or omission which did not constitute a penal offence, under

national or international law, at the time when it was committed. Nor shall a heavier penalty be imposed than the one that was applicable at the time the penal offence was committed.

Article 12.
No one shall be subjected to arbitrary interference with his privacy, family, home or correspondence, nor to attacks upon his honour and reputation. Everyone has the right to the protection of the law against such interference or attacks.

Article 13.
(1) Everyone has the right to freedom of movement and residence within the borders of each state.
(2) Everyone has the right to leave any country, including his own, and to return to his country.

Article 14.
(1) Everyone has the right to seek and to enjoy in other countries asylum from persecution.
(2) This right may not be invoked in the case of prosecutions genuinely arising from non-political crimes or from acts contrary to the purposes and principles of the United Nations.

Article 15.
(1) Everyone has the right to a nationality.
(2) No one shall be arbitrarily deprived of his nationality nor denied the right to change his nationality.

Article 16.
(1) Men and women of full age, without any limitation due to race, nationality or religion, have the right to marry and to found a family. They are entitled to equal rights as to marriage, during marriage and at its dissolution.
(2) Marriage shall be entered into only with the free and full consent of the intending spouses.
(3) The family is the natural and fundamental group unit of society and is entitled to protection by society and the State.

Article 17.

(1) Everyone has the right to own property alone as well as in association with others.

(2) No one shall be arbitrarily deprived of his property.

Article 18.

Everyone has the right to freedom of thought, conscience and religion; this right includes freedom to change his religion or belief, and freedom, either alone or in community with others and in public or private, to manifest his religion or belief in teaching, practice, worship and observance.

Article 19.

Everyone has the right to freedom of opinion and expression; this right includes freedom to hold opinions without interference and to seek, receive and impart information and ideas through any media and regardless of frontiers.

Article 20.

(1) Everyone has the right to freedom of peaceful assembly and association.

(2) No one may be compelled to belong to an association.

Article 21.

(1) Everyone has the right to take part in the government of his country, directly or through freely chosen representatives.

(2) Everyone has the right of equal access to public service in his country.

(3) The will of the people shall be the basis of the authority of government; this will shall be expressed in periodic and genuine elections which shall be by universal and equal suffrage and shall be held by secret vote or by equivalent free voting procedures.

Article 22.

Everyone, as a member of society, has the right to social security and is entitled to realization, through national effort and international cooperation and in accordance with the organization and resources of each

State, of the economic, social and cultural rights indispensable for his dignity and the free development of his personality.

Article 23.

(1) Everyone has the right to work, to free choice of employment, to just and favourable conditions of work and to protection against unemployment.

(2) Everyone, without any discrimination, has the right to equal pay for equal work.

(3) Everyone who works has the right to just and favourable remuneration ensuring for himself and his family an existence worthy of human dignity, and supplemented, if necessary, by other means of social protection.

(4) Everyone has the right to form and to join trade unions for the protection of his interests.

Article 24.

Everyone has the right to rest and leisure, including reasonable limitation of working hours and periodic holidays with pay.

Article 25.

(1) Everyone has the right to a standard of living adequate for the health and well-being of himself and of his family, including food, clothing, housing and medical care and necessary social services, and the right to security in the event of unemployment, sickness, disability, widowhood, old age or other lack of livelihood in circumstances beyond his control.

(2) Motherhood and childhood are entitled to special care and assistance. All children, whether born in or out of wedlock, shall enjoy the same social protection.

Article 26.

(1) Everyone has the right to education. Education shall be free, at least in the elementary and fundamental stages. Elementary education shall be compulsory. Technical and professional education shall be made generally available and higher education shall be equally accessible to all on the basis of merit.

(2) Education shall be directed to the full development of the human personality and to the strengthening of respect for human rights and fundamental freedoms. It shall promote understanding, tolerance and friendship among all nations, racial or religious groups, and shall further the activities of the United Nations for the maintenance of peace.

(3) Parents have a prior right to choose the kind of education that shall be given to their children.

Article 27.

(1) Everyone has the right freely to participate in the cultural life of the community, to enjoy the arts and to share in scientific advancement and its benefits.

(2) Everyone has the right to the protection of the moral and material interests resulting from any scientific, literary or artistic production of which he is the author.

Article 28.

Everyone is entitled to a social and international order in which the rights and freedoms set forth in this Declaration can be fully realized.

Article 29.

(1) Everyone has duties to the community in which alone the free and full development of his personality is possible.

(2) In the exercise of his rights and freedoms, everyone shall be subject only to such limitations as are determined by law solely for the purpose of securing due recognition and respect for the rights and freedoms of others and of meeting the just requirements of morality, public order and the general welfare in a democratic society.

(3) These rights and freedoms may in no case be exercised contrary to the purposes and principles of the United Nations.

Article 30.

Nothing in this Declaration may be interpreted as implying for any State, group or person any right to engage in any activity or to perform any act aimed at the destruction of any of the rights and freedoms set forth herein.

UN Member States

The 192 member states, with the date on which each joined the United Nations:

Afghanistan, November 19, 1946
Albania, December 14, 1955
Algeria, October 8, 1962
Andorra, July 28, 1993
Angola, December 1, 1976
Antigua and Barbuda, November 11, 1981
Argentina, October 24, 1945
Armenia, March 2, 1992
Australia, November 1, 1945
Austria, December 14, 1955
Azerbaijan, March 2, 1992
Bahamas, September 18, 1973
Bahrain, September 21, 1971
Bangladesh, September 17, 1974
Barbados, December 9, 1966

Belarus, October 24, 1945
Belgium, December 27, 1945
Belize, September 25, 1981
Benin, September 20, 1960
Bhutan, September 21, 1971
Bolivia, November 14, 1945
Bosnia and Herzegovina, May 22, 1992
Botswana, October 17, 1966
Brazil, October 24, 1945
Brunei Darussalam, September 21, 1984
Bulgaria, December 14, 1955
Burkina Faso, September 20, 1960
Burundi, September 18, 1962
Cambodia, December 14, 1955
Cameroon, September 20, 1960
Canada, November 9, 1945
Cape Verde, September 16, 1975
Central African Republic, September 20, 1960
Chad, September 20, 1960
Chile, October 24, 1945
China, October 24, 1945
Colombia, November 5, 1945
Comoros, November 12, 1975
Congo, Democratic Republic of the, September 20, 1960
Congo, Republic of the, September 20, 1960
Costa Rica, November 2, 1945
Côte d'Ivoire, September 20, 1960
Croatia, May 22, 1992
Cuba, October 24, 1945
Cyprus, September 20, 1960
Czech Republic, January 19, 1993
Denmark, October 24, 1945
Djibouti, September 20, 1977
Dominica, December 18, 1978
Dominican Republic, October 24, 1945

Ecuador, December 21, 1945
Egypt, October 24, 1945
El Salvador, October 24, 1945
Equatorial Guinea, November 12, 1968
Eritrea, May 28, 1993
Estonia, September 17, 1991
Ethiopia, November 13, 1945
Fiji, October 13, 1970
Finland, December 14, 1955
France, October 24, 1945
Gabon, September 20, 1960
Gambia, September 21, 1965
Georgia, July 31, 1992
Germany, September 18, 1973
Ghana, March 8, 1957
Greece, October 25, 1945
Grenada, September 17, 1974
Guatemala, November 21, 1945
Guinea, December 12, 1958
Guinea-Bissau, September 17, 1974
Guyana, September 20, 1966
Haiti, October 24, 1945
Honduras, December 17, 1945
Hungary, December 14, 1955
Iceland, November 19, 1946
India, October 30, 1945
Indonesia, September 28, 1950
Iran, Islamic Republic of, October 24, 1945
Iraq, December 21, 1945
Ireland, December 14, 1955
Israel, May 11, 1949
Italy, December 14, 1955
Jamaica, September 18, 1962
Japan, December 18, 1956
Jordan, December 14, 1955

Kazakhstan, March 2, 1992
Kenya, December 16, 1963
Kiribati, September 14, 1999
Korea, Democratic People's Republic of, September 17, 1991
Korea, Republic of, September 17, 1991
Kuwait, May 14, 1963
Kyrgyzstan, March 2, 1992
Lao People's Democratic Republic, December 14, 1955
Latvia, September 17, 1991
Lebanon, October 24, 1945
Lesotho, October 17, 1966
Liberia, November 2, 1945
Libyan Arab Jamahiriya, December 14, 1955
Liechtenstein, September 18, 1990
Lithuania, September 17, 1991
Luxembourg, October 24, 1945
Macedonia, former Yugoslav Republic of, April 8, 1993
Madagascar, September 20, 1960
Malawi, December 1, 1964
Malaysia, September 17, 1957
Maldives, September 21, 1965
Mali, September 28, 1960
Malta, December 1, 1964
Marshall Islands, September 17, 1991
Mauritania, October 27, 1961
Mauritius, April 24, 1968
Mexico, November 7, 1945
Micronesia, Federated States of, September 17, 1991
Moldava, Republic of, March 2, 1992
Monaco, May 28, 1993
Mongolia, October 27, 1961
Montenegro, June 28, 2006
Morocco, November 12, 1956
Mozambique, September 16, 1975
Myanmar, April 19, 1948
Namibia, April 23, 1990

Nauru, September 14, 1999
Nepal, December 14, 1955
Netherlands, December 10, 1945
New Zealand, October 24, 1945
Nicaragua, October 24, 1945
Niger, September 20, 1960
Nigeria, October 7, 1960
Norway, November 27, 1945
Oman, October 7, 1971
Pakistan, September 30, 1947
Palau, December 15, 1994
Panama, November 13, 1945
Papua New Guinea, October 10, 1975
Paraguay, October 24, 1945
Peru, October 31, 1945
Philippines, October 24, 1945
Poland, October 24, 1945
Portugal, December 14, 1955
Qatar, September 21, 1971
Romania, December 14, 1955
Russian Federation, October 24, 1945
Rwanda, September 18, 1962
Saint Kitts and Nevis, September 23, 1983
Saint Lucia, September 18, 1979
Saint Vincent and the Grenadines, September 16, 1980
Samoa, December 15, 1976
San Marino, March 2, 1992
São Tomé and Príncipe, September 16, 1975
Saudi Arabia, October 24, 1945
Senegal, September 28, 1960
Serbia, November 1, 2000
Seychelles, September 21, 1976
Sierra Leone, September 27, 1961
Singapore, September 21, 1965
Slovakia, January 19, 1993
Slovenia, May 22, 1992

Solomon Islands, September 19, 1978
Somalia, September 20, 1960
South Africa, November 7, 1945
Spain, December 14, 1955
Sri Lanka, December 14, 1955
Sudan, November 12, 1956
Suriname, December 4, 1975
Swaziland, September 24, 1968
Sweden, November 19, 1946
Switzerland, September 10, 2002
Syrian Arab Republic, October 24, 1945
Tajikistan, March 2, 1992
Tanzania, United Republic of, December 14, 1961
Thailand, December 16, 1946
Timor-Leste, September 27, 2002
Togo, September 20, 1960
Tonga, September 14, 1999
Trinidad and Tobago, September 18, 1962
Tunisia, November 12, 1956
Turkey, October 24, 1945
Turkmenistan, March 2, 1992
Tuvalu, September 5, 2000
Uganda, October 24, 1962
Ukraine, October 24, 1945
United Arab Emirates, December 9, 1971
United Kingdom of Great Britain and Northern Ireland, October 24, 1945
United States of America, October 24, 1945
Uruguay, December 18, 1945
Uzbekistan, March 2, 1992
Vanuatu, September 15, 1981
Venezuela, Bolivarian Republic of, November 15, 1945
Viet Nam, September 20, 1977
Yemen, September 30, 1947
Zambia, December 1, 1964
Zimbabwe, August 25, 1980

Model UN: How to Participate

The following questions and answers are selected and reprinted from "Model UN," on the web site of the United Nations Association of the United States, www.unausa.org.

Q: What is Model United Nations?

A: Model United Nations is a simulation of the UN General Assembly and other multilateral bodies. In Model UN, students step into the shoes of ambassadors from UN member states to debate current issues on the organization's agenda. While playing their roles as ambassadors, student "delegates" make speeches, prepare draft resolutions, negotiate with allies and adversaries, resolve conflicts, and navigate the Model UN conference rules of procedure—all in the interest of mobilizing "international cooperation" to resolve problems that affect countries all over the world.

Before playing out their ambassadorial roles in a Model UN simulation, students research the issue that their committee will address. Model UN participants learn how the international community acts on its concerns about topics including peace and security, human rights, the environment, food and hunger, economic development and globalization. Model UN delegates also look closely at the needs, goals and foreign policies of the countries they will represent at the event. The insights they gain from their exploration of history, geography, culture, economics and science contribute to the authenticity of the simulation when the role playing gets under way. The delegates' in-depth knowledge of their countries guarantees a lively and memorable experience.

Q: What is the relationship of UNA-USA to Model United Nations?

A: UNA-USA, a nonprofit, nonpartisan national organization with a network of more than 175 community-based chapters and divisions, has been a driving force behind Model UN education since the inception of its predecessor organization, the American Association for the United Nations, in 1943. Model UN is neither a UN nor a UNA creation, and it is not officially owned by any individual organization. The Model UN program in the United States is actually a decentralized community that is driven predominately by its student participants.

UNA-USA strives to act as a clearing house for Model UN resources for participants and organizers. UNA-USA has created a library of Model UN publications including the Guide to Delegate Preparation, the *Global Classrooms*® Program curricular units, the Model UN for Everyone video and How to Plan a Model United Nations Conference. UNA-USA also hosts over 25 conferences a year in cities around the world.

Q: Who participates in Model United Nations?

A: The popularity of Model UN continues to grow and more than 400,000 middle school, high school and college/university students worldwide participate every year. Many of today's leaders in law, government, business and the arts participated in Model UN during their academic careers:

- US Supreme Court Justice Stephen Breyer
- Former World Court Justice Stephen M. Schwebel
- ABC's This Week anchor George Stephanopoulos
- Former first-daughter Chelsea Clinton
- Under-Secretary General for Public Information, Kiyotaka Akasaka

- UN Secretary-General, Ban Ki-Moon
- Actor Samuel L. Jackson
- Ryan Seacrest from American Idol
- Rainn Wilson-Dwight from "The Office"

Q: What is a Model UN delegate?
A: A Model UN delegate is a student who assumes the role of an ambassador to the United Nations in a Model UN simulation. Prior to a conference or event, a Model UN delegate does not need extensive experience in international relations. Anyone can participate in Model UN, so long as they have the ambition to learn something new and to work with people to try and make a difference in the world. Model UN students tend to go on to become great leaders in politics, law, business, education and medicine, such as the people mentioned above.

Q: What is a Model UN conference?
A: Some Model UN exercises take place in the classroom and others are school-wide. Model UN events that are regional, national or international are called conferences. Conferences are much larger, with participants from all over the United States and the world. More than one million people have participated in Model UN conferences around the world since they became popular over 50 years ago. Today there are more than 400 conferences that take place in 52 countries. Conferences can have as few as 30 students or as many as 3,000.

Q: Where can I find information about conferences in my area?
A: For dates and more information on conferences all over the world, visit UNA-USA's Model UN Conference Calendar. If you are a conference organizer, you can also input your conference's information to be accessed by everyone. In addition, you can join our mun-e-news yahoo group to receive messages regarding Model UN conferences. Lastly, you can simply search for "Model UN conferences" and your location on the internet.

Q: How do I decide which Model UN conferences to attend?
A: For Model UN groups that are just beginning, it's best to attend smaller Model UN conferences that are aimed at first-time participants. Smaller conferences provide more opportunities for you to interact with other delegates and to have your voice heard. Consider

whether your Model UN team will be comfortable in a situation where there are 200+ students in a committee room.

Q: Where can my organization get the funds to attend a Model UN conference?

A: Because many Model UN conferences are held at colleges and hotels, fees can range from $5 to $250+ per delegate. These fees usually do not include transportation, meals, or lodging. In a few cases, meals and lodging are covered. Some conferences offer an early-registration discount, while others have late fees. Many Model UN groups request funds through their school's administration to cover transportation and conference costs. Other groups apply for scholarships, but these are usually limited to groups traveling abroad. Model UN clubs can request funds through their local UNA-USA chapter. Groups should also try local organizations such as Rotary and Lions Clubs for support. Most groups do a lot of their own fundraising through monthly group activities, dance-a-thons, bake sales, car washes and sporting events.

Q: How should I prepare for my Model UN conference?

A: Researching is the first and most important step in preparing for a conference. Not only is it necessary to have a grasp on information about the country you are representing and its position on the policies being discussed, it is also important to understand the UN body that your committee is representing. For an overview of research suggestions, as well as useful links, visit our Research Overview from the Model UN Preparation Guide.

Q: What is a position paper and how do I write one?

A: Before attending a conference, it is necessary to have a clear understanding about the workings of your country, as well as its position on the issues that are being discussed. Most conferences will even require a position paper in advance to ensure that delegates have properly researched their country. Position papers should contain your country's relation to the topic, as well as its suggestions for how to solve the issues discussed. For more information about position paper form, as well as a sample position paper, visit the Position Paper section from the Model UN Preparation Guide.

Q: How do I write a resolution?

A: During a committee session resolutions are essential to promote debate and create solutions to issues that are being discussed. Resolutions not only acknowledge the issues that are being debated, but they also present a series of steps that can be taken resolve the conflict. Writing resolutions can be challenging since they must appeal to a broad range of members with differing concerns if they are going to be successfully passed. For information on correct format and helpful tips, visit the Resolutions section from the Model UN Preparation Guide.

Q: How does my team register for a Model UN Conference?

A: The UNA-USA Model UN Calendar is designed to make it as easy as possible for you to select the conference best suited to your schedule, financial resources and location. To register for a Model UN Conference, your team should:

- Select the dates and location of the Model UN conference appropriate to your group's academic level and financial resources. Also, set goals on what you would like to achieve by attending a particular Model UN conference;
- Write to the Secretary-General or contact person for the Model UN conference to request registration forms, and if you wish, contact information for a faculty advisor or student who attended the conference the year before. Many conferences have websites that provide a good look into the size and scope of a conference. Some sites even have registration forms on-line;
- Keep in mind that many conferences are student-run. If you do not receive your information within a reasonable amount of time, a quick phone call can get things on track;
- Once you have received conference registration forms, complete and return the requested information and fees. Your group will soon receive confirmation of registration and a country assignment as well as a conference schedule, background materials and hotel information. Remember to keep a copy of all materials and checks sent to conference organizers.

Q: How do we select a country?

A: When registering for a Model UN conference, participants will usually be asked to indicate which countries they want to role-play at the conference. Although there are 192 countries to choose from, many schools compete for the 15 countries on the Security Council, especially the five permanent members with veto power: China, France, the Russian Federation, the United Kingdom, and the United States. New teams should request mid-sized countries, as they play an integral role in debate but are not overwhelming. It is worth noting, however, that in the General Assembly, the Economic and Social Council, and most other UN committees and agencies, the principle of sovereign equality governs the proceedings. This means each member state has one vote. Even the "smallest" member state not only has an important role to play, but can sometimes wield considerable influence. Therefore, bear in mind that size and power are not the only important criteria for choosing an interesting country to represent.

SOURCES

The sources for this book are available in libraries and on the Internet, except for the interviews that I conducted with diplomats, UN officials, scholars, and others. Unless mentioned in the text below, quotations in the book come from these interviews.

For basic information about the UN system I relied heavily on the web sites of the UN and its various organs, agencies, commissions, and programs. I also consulted the standard reference work by the UN, *Basic Facts about the United Nations* (New York: United Nations, 2004). US State Department reports, available on the State Department's web site (www.state .gov), provided detailed information about important aspects of the UN. The first is the *US Report to the UN Counterterrorism Committee,* December 19, 2001, which describes the US government's actions taken in compliance with Security Council Resolution 1373, against terrorism. Extremely helpful were the *Eighteenth* (2000) and *Twenty-fifth Annual Report on Voting Practices in the UN* (2007), which analyze how UN member states voted in comparison with US voting patterns. Finally, *US Participation in the United Nations* (2000 and 2006) minutely describes the relationship of the US with all parts of the UN system, including financial assessments and contributions.

I used the United Nations Foundation's web site to access UNWire, an electronic database that contains English-language news stories about the UN for about the past three years. The entries provide summaries and in many cases full text of the articles. I have not referenced UNWire at each point where I used it, but I acknowledge here that it was an invaluable tool. In those instances where I quoted from or relied heavily on news stories, these are noted below, by chapter, in the order in which they appear.

Chapter 1.   The epigraph is from President-Elect Barack Obama's speech on December 1, 2008, naming his national security team. All quotations in the book by Susan E. Rice are taken from her confirmation hearing in January 2009.

Chapter 2.   For the Charter, see Marjorie Ann Browne and Kennon H. Nakamura, *United Nations Funding: Congressional Issues, Updated February 1, 2008* (Washington, DC: Congressional Research Service, 2008), 26. Eleanor Roosevelt's role in writing the Universal Declaration appears in Joseph Lash, *Eleanor: The Years Alone* (New York: Konecky and Knoecky, 1972), 36. Brian Urquhart's statement on the declaration's importance is from his interviews at the University of California, Berkeley.

Chapter 3.   The *Economist* article on Ban Ki-moon, "The Rewards of Beavering Away," January 3, 2008, provides a good overview of the new secretary-general's first year in office. On the "opacity" of the selection process, see "Opaque Selection Process Suits a Unique, Vaguely Defined Office," *Disarmament Times*, Fall 2006, 4.

Chapter 5.   For the council's growing activity, see Edward C. Luck, *UN Security Council: Practice and Promise* (London: Routledge, 2006), 17. His comments immediately below that are drawn from my interview of him, however. Sanctions were the topic of a UN-sponsored meeting at which Ban Ki-moon spoke: *Enhancing the Implementation of United Nations Security Council Sanctions: A Symposium, 30 April 2007* (New York: United Nations, 2007). The quotation about the US government's favorable view of sanctions comes from *US Participation in the UN*, 2006, 54. The description of a SC debate on the role of women comes from U.S. State Department, *US Participation in the UN, 2006*, 64.

Chapter 9.   The epigraph is taken from Morton Abramowitz and Thomas Pickering, "Making Intervention Work: Improving the UN's Ability to Act," *Foreign Affairs* 87 (2008): 100–109. The recent State Department Report is *US Participation in the UN*, 2006, 49. For the Peacebuilding Commission, see remarks in "Interview with Necla Tschirgi," *UN Reform Watch* , December 22, 2005. A BBC News report from July 2007 was helpful for the section on Ethiopia/Eritrea and the village of Badme; and an AP story of August 8, 2007, described allegations that the Eritreans were supporting Muslim militants in Somalia. Khalilzad's statement that peacekeeping should not be a substitute for finding a solution appears in Merle D. Kellerhals, "UN Looking for Ways to Enhance African Peacekeeping," *Peace and Security,* April 22, 2008. The figures for sexual assaults involving peacekeepers are from US State Department, *US Participation in the UN, 2006,* 50. For the two favorable US government reports on peacekeeping, see www.gao.gov/new.items/d06331.pdf; and www.betterworldcampaign.org/pd/bwc—factsheet—peace keeping—arrears—0307.pdf. The Human Security Report analysis is available at www.humansecurityreport.info.

Chapter 10. A useful article was David Cortwright, "Can the UN Battle Terrorism Effectively?" *USA Today Magazine,* January 2005. Annan made his comments about nuclear proliferation and disarmament at Princeton University on November 28, 2006. The discussion of Security Council Resolution 1540 comes mainly from a report by Peter Burian, chairman of the 1540 Committee: "Global Initiatives to Combat WMD," May 16, 2007. The comments about the UN as terrorist target come in part from Colum Lynch, "UN Insignia Emerges as a Global Target for Al-Qaeda Attacks," *Washington Post,* December 25, 2007; and a Reuters story, "UN 'Has Become an Enemy,'" February 29, 2008.

Chapter 11 China's emergence as the main carbon dioxide emitter is from Alex Morales, "China Becomes World's Biggest Carbon Dioxide Emitter (Update 1)," *Bloomberg News,* June 20, 2007. Ban Ki-moon's July 2007 remarks appear in Terence Chea, "UN Chief Ban Ki-moon Visits California," *Washington Post,* July 27, 2007. The discussion about Bali and Bangkok is from a CNN report, "World Summit Turns to Greenhouse Gases," March 31, 2008. Ban Ki-moon's address at the Third Annual Summit on Climate Risk is described by Joy Cook, "Climate Change: Beyond Bali, UN Keeps up Pressure," *UNA-USA Newsletter, E-News,* February 19, 2008.

Chapter 12. The quoted phrase on the ICC's first case, in 2007, comes from comments by Philippe Kirsch to the UN General Assembly on November 1, 2007. On the significance of Bellinger's speech, see also Sue Pleming, "US Takes More Pragmatic View of World Court," Reuters, May 7, 2008. For the HRC, see Suzanne Nosel, "Human Rights Council Will Prove Its Worth in Coming Weeks," *New Republic,* June 19, 2007. David Malone, in a letter to the *Toronto Star,* January 5, 2000, praised Annan for commissioning the report on the Rwanda genocide. Ban Ki-moon's willingness to advance difficult issues receives comment in "The Rewards of Beavering Away," *Economist,* January 3, 2008.

Chapter 13.   Khalilzad's statement in the epigraph is from the UNA-USA web site. The discussion about how regular assessments are calculated benefited from the State Department's *U.S. Participation in the UN, 2006*, 148. The budget process discussion relies in part on fact sheets that Robert W. Hsu prepared for UNA-USA. Speculation on causes for the rapid rise in UN budgets appears in Colum Lynch, "Expenses at U.N. Balloon 25 Percent," *Washington Post,* March 21, 2008. The Japanese proposal for a 3 or 5 percent floor for the P5 is described by Brett D. Schaefer and Janice A. Smith, "The U.S. Should Support Japan's Call to Revise the UN Scale of Assessments," *Web Memo 1017* (Washington, DC: Heritage Foundation), March 18, 2006. The data on U.S. financial support for the UN in fiscal year 2006 comes from US Department of State, "U.S. Financial Contributions to the United Nations System," September 20, 2007. The discussion of arrears benefited from two reports by the Global Policy Forum, "Regular Budget Assessments and Payments, 2007," and "U.S. vs. Total Debt to the UN: 2007." The decision by New York City to stop UN tours for schoolchildren is reported by Jennifer Peltz of Associated Press in an article of September 10, 2008.

Chapter 14.   The dollar amounts for Oil-for-Food during its existence come from a study by the US Government Accountability Office, "Lessons Learned from Oil for Food Program Indicate Need to Strengthen UN Internal Controls and Oversight Activities," April 25, 2006. The quotation by Hillary Rodham Clinton on the United Nations comes from a statement she issued during her presidential campaign in 2008. The Luers interview with Volcker, "Oil-for-Food Program Revisited—A Conversation with Paul Volcker," was published by the *Interdependent,* www.theinterdependent.org. The discussion of the Procurement Task Force and Christopher Burnham comes from Robert W. Hsu's "American UN Official Steps Down; Post Allocation May Threaten UN Reform," *UNA-USA Publications,* December 5, 2007, and Lydia Swart's "UN Will Continue to Fight Corruption in 2008," *UNA-USA Publications,* January 8, 2008.

Chapter 16.   The Adopt-A-Minefield program is described by Kevin Newman of ABC in UNWire, December 10, 1999.

Appendixes.   The appendixes are drawn from the UN's Office of Public Inquiries.

UN and Other Web Sites

UN homepage: www.un.org
UN cyberschoolbus: www.un.org/Pubs/CyberSchoolBus/
UN main bodies: www.un.org/aboutun/mainbodies.htm
UN news: www.un.org/news
UN NGOs: www.un.org/esa/coordination/ngo/
UN organization web site locator: www.unsystem.org
UN permanent missions: www.un.it

American Enterprise Institute: www.aei.org
Better World Campaign: www.betterworldfund.org
Center for UN Reform: www.centerforunreform.org
Center on International Cooperation: www.cic.nyu.edu
Council on Foreign Relations: www.cfr.org
Foreign Policy Association: www.fpa.org
Heritage Foundation: www.heritagefoundation.org
International Crisis Group: www.intl-crisis-group.org
International Peace Institute: www.ipinst.org
Maxims News Network: www.maximsnews.com
Model UN: www.unausa.org/mun

National Committee on American Foreign Policy: www.ncafp.org
National Model UN: www.nmun.org
Security Council Report: www.securitycouncilreport.org
UN Association of the United States: www.unausa.org
UN Foundation: www.unfoundation.org
UN Watch: www.unwatch.org
UN Wire: www.unwire.org
US Participation in the United Nations: www.state.gov/p/io/conrpt/partic/
US State Department: www.state.gov
World Affairs Councils of America: www.worldaffairscouncils.org
World Federation of UN Associations: www.wfuna.org

General

Annan, Kofi A. *We the Peoples: The Role of the United Nations in the Twenty-First Century.* New York: United Nations, 2000.

Bolton, John. *Surrender Is Not an Option: Defending America at the United Nations.* New York: Threshold Editions, 2007.

Boutros-Ghali, B. *Unvanquished: A US-UN Saga.* New York: Random House, 1999.

Coicaud, Jean-Marc. *National Interest and International Solidarity: Particular and Universal Ethics in International Life.* New York: United Nations University Press, 2007.

Doyle, Michael W., and Nicholas Sambanis. *Making War and Building Peace: United Nations Peace Operations.* Princeton, NJ: Princeton University Press, 2006.

Garekhan, Chinmaya R. *The Horseshoe Table: An Inside View of the UN Security Council.* New Delhi: Dorling Kindersley (India), 2006.

Hoopes, T. *FDR and the Creation of the United Nations.* New Haven and London: Yale University Press, 2000.

Kennedy, Paul. *The Parliament of Man: The Past, Present, and Future of the United Nations.* New York: Random House, 2006.

Krasno, Jean E., and James S. Sutterlin. *The United Nations and Iraq: Defanging the Viper.* Westport, CT: Praeger, 2003.

Leslie, Scott A., ed. *A Guide to Delegate Preparation: A Model United Nations Handbook.* New York: United Nations Association of the United States of America, 2004.

Luck, Edward C. *UN Security Council: Practice and Promise.* New York, Routledge, 2006.

Malone, David M., ed. *The UN Security Council: From the Cold War to the Twenty-First Century.* Boulder, CO: Lynne Rienner, 2004.

Meisler, Stanley. *United Nations: The First Fifty Years.* New York: Atlantic Monthly, 1997.

Mingst, Karen A., and Magaret P. Karns. *The United Nations in the Twenty-First Century (Dilemmas in World Politics).* Boulder, CO: Westview, 2006.

Russett, Bruce, ed. *The Once and Future Security Council.* New York: St. Martin's, 1997.

Schlesinger, Stephen. *Act of Creation: The Founding of the United Nations.* Boulder, CO: Westview, 2003.

Traub, James. *The Best Intentions: Kofi Annan and the UN in the Era of American World Power.* New York: Farrar, Straus and Giroux, 2006.

United Nations. *Basic Facts about the United Nations.* New York: United Nations, 2004.

US Department of State, www.state.gov. *US Participation in the UN, Yearly Reports.* 1990–2006.

——. *Eighteenth Annual Report on Voting Practices in the UN, 2000.*

——. *Twenty-Fifth Annual Report on Voting Practices in the UN, 2007.*

——. *US Report to the UN Counterterrorism Committee, December 19, 2001.*

Weiss, Thomas G., and Sam Daws, eds. *The Oxford Handbook on the United Nations.* New York: Oxford University Press, 2007.

Weiss, Thomas G., and D. P. Forsythe. *The United Nations and Changing World Politics.* Boulder,CO: Westview, 2007.

Humanitarian Aid

Beristain, Carlos Martin, and M. Brinton Lykes. *Humanitarian Aid Work: A Critical Approach.* Philadelphia: University of Pennsylvania Press, 2008.

Forman, S., and S. Patrick, eds. *Good Intentions: Pledges of Aid for Post-Conflict Recovery.* Boulder, CO: Lynne Rienner, 2000.

Lischer, Sarah Kenyon. *Dangerous Sanctuaries: Refugee Camps, Civil War, and the Dilemmas of Humanitarian Aid.* Cornell Studies in Security Affairs. Ithaca, NY: Cornell University Press, 2005.

Martin, Francisco Forrest, Stephen J. Schnably, Richard Wilson, Jonathan Simon, and Mark Tushnet. *International Human Rights and Humanitarian*

Law: Treaties, Cases, and Analysis. New York: Cambridge University Press, 2006.

Richardson, Nan, ed. *Pandemic: Facing AIDS / Essays by Kofi Annan.* New York: Turnaround, 2003.

Human Rights

Amnesty International. *The State of the World's Human Rights.* Published annually.

Human Rights Watch. *World Report: Human Rights Watch.* New York: Human Rights Watch, published annually.

Steidl, Brian, and Gretchen Steidle Wallace. *The Devil Came on Horseback: Bearing Witness to the Genocide in Darfur.* New York: Public Affairs, 2007.

Peace and Peacekeeping

Albright, Madeleine. *Focus on the Issues: Building Peace and Security around the World.* Washington, DC: US Department of State, 2000.

Annan, Kofi A. *Prevention of Armed Conflict: Report of the Secretary-General.* New York: United Nations, 2002.

Baylis, John, Steve Smith, and Patricia Owens, eds. *The Globalization of World Politics.* New York: Oxford University Press, 2008.

Chollet, Derek, with a foreword by Richard Holbrooke. *The Road to the Dayton Accords: A Study of American Statecraft.* New York: Palgrave Macmillan, 2005.

Holbrooke, Richard. *To End a War.* New York: Modern Library, 1999.

Holzgrefe, J. L., and Robert O. Keohane, eds. *Humanitarian Intervention: Ethical, Legal, and Political Dilemmas.* Cambridge: Cambridge University Press, 2003.

International Development Research Centre. *The Responsibility to Protect: Report of the International Commission on Intervention and State Sovereignty.* Ottawa, Canada: International Development Research Centre, December 2001.

Jarstad, Anna K., and Timothy D. Sisk, eds. *From War to Democracy: Dilemmas of Peacebuilding.* New York: Cambridge University Press, 2008.

Jeong, Ho-Won, ed. *Approaches to Peacebuilding.* New York: Palgrave Macmillan, 2002.

Keating, Thomas F., and W. Andy Knight, eds. *Building Sustainable Peace.* New York: United Nations University Press, 2004.

Laurenti, Jeffrey, and Carl Robichaud, eds. *Making the Nuclear Impasse: New Prospects for Security against Weapons Threats.* New York: Century Foundation, 2007.

Mason, T. David, and James D. Meernik, eds. *Conflict Prevention and Peacebuilding in Post-War Societies: Sustaining the Peace.* New York: Routledge, 2006.

Paris, Roland. *At War's End: Building Peace after Civil Conflict.* New York: Cambridge University Press, 2004.

Stromseth, Jane, David Wippman, and Rosa Brooks. *Can Might Make Rights? Building the Rule of Law after Military Interventions.* New York: Cambridge University Press, 2006.

United Nations. *An Agenda for Peace: Preventive Diplomacy, Peacemaking and Peacekeeping.* A/47/277-S/24111, 17 June 1992. Full text available at http://www.un.org/Docs/SG/agpeace.html.

——. "Report of the Panel on United Nations Peace Operations." A/55/305, S/2000/809, 2000. Full text available at http://www.un.org/peace/ reports/peace operations.

——. *UN Peacekeeping: Fifty Years (1948–1998).* New York: United Nations, 1998.

United Nations Association of the United States. *The Preparedness Gap: Making Peace Operations Work in the Twenty-First Century: A Policy Report of the United Nations Association of the United States of America.* New York: United Nations Association of the United States, 2000.